DANGEROUS HOUSE, DANGEROUS HOME

A GUIDE FOR HOME OWNERSHIP

G. STEVEN SCHREFFLER

Visit our website at
www.StillwaterPress.com
for more information.

First Stillwater River Publications Edition

ISBN: 978-1-955123-70-9

1 2 3 4 5 6 7 8 9 10
Written by G. Steven Schreffler
Published by Stillwater River Publications,
Pawtucket, RI, USA.

Publisher's Cataloging-In-Publication Data
(Prepared by The Donohue Group, Inc.)

Names: Schreffler, G. Steven, author.
Title: Dangerous house, dangerous home : a guide for home ownership /
G. Steven Schreffler.
Description: First Stillwater River Publications edition. |
Pawtucket, RI, USA : Stillwater River Publications, [2022]
Identifiers: ISBN 9781955123709
Subjects: LCSH: Dwellings--Inspection--Handbooks, manuals, etc. |
House buying--Handbooks, manuals, etc. |
Home ownership--Handbooks, manuals, etc.
Classification: LCC TH4817.5 .S37 2022 | DDC 643.12--dc23

The views and opinions expressed
in this book are solely those of the author
and do not necessarily reflect the views
and opinions of the publisher.

*This book is dedicated to my beautiful wife Lynne
and my eldest son Ryan.*

*Their love and support over these many years
has meant the world to me, and due to all their support
for me I was able to write this book.*

CONTENTS

BUYING A HOME
INTRODUCTION

My career includes 38 years of law enforcement and over 25 years of self-defense training. I am a registered contractor and Certified Home Inspector with over 45 years of construction experience, over five years of commercial construction inspections for banks and lending institutions, and a real estate investor. I worked for over three years designing security and video systems for high-end homes for the largest security company in the country. I also have 20 years of childcare education and owned and operated a childcare facility.

Three years ago, I decided to become a personal security consultant and utilize all this experience to keep families safe in their own homes. This has since been expanded to developing seminars to keep real estate agents and brokers safe when showing homes and during open houses for their clients. I have also been approached by the State of Rhode Island Constables Association to develop a training program to keep their constables safe when delivering usually bad news.

This book, unlike any other books out there, will not show you how to fix your credit score, or how to buy your first home, or home improvements and home maintenance. It is written so that I may share all my experiences in all areas of my career in helping people with one of the most important endeavors in their lives: buying and owning a home. This book is also a great resource for real estate agents and brokers. If you're anything like me, well, I don't like surprises, especially if they are going to cost me money. I highly suggest you read this book as it will help you understand what you're about to pursue.

The first section of this book is to give you a better perspective on what to look for that may be a future potential problem. It's written from a home inspector's perspective, a law enforcer's perspective, and a personal safety consultant's perspective to keep you and your family safe.

Over the many years of experience in so many areas, I have seen many mistakes and oversights made that could potentially cause harm, both physical and financial, to a family that buys a house. I have also seen and experienced many families going through situations that could have been avoided had they had the knowledge on what to look for before they bought their home.

I have also met and worked with many existing homeowners on how to keep themselves and their families safe in their home. Families, young and old, can have many different challenges; and having knowledge on how to keep your home safe and not dangerous is extremely important.

Equipment located in the home is being made cheaper with planned obsolescence. Fires start within walls if the wiring is faulty or chewed by unwanted four-legged visitors. Electrical outlets and light switches are mass produced, very inexpensive, and break very easily. I've seen toasters fail, dehumidifiers short out and catch fire, light fixtures improperly installed and shorting out, ground fault circuit interrupters (GFCI) fail, extension cords and multi-outlet strips overtaxed which can start fires. I've seen oil burners blow back and spread soot all over the home, water lines burst and flood houses, sewers back up and destroy finished basements, and carbon monoxide detectors going off due to faulty or blocked vents.

I have learned over the years that just giving someone knowledge is hard for them to remember; sharing that knowledge in the form of stories and pictures helps them to retain that knowledge. I will try to do both and show you how to have a Safe House and a Safe Home!

Dangerous House—Dangerous Home is designed not only to keep you from buying a dangerous house and show you how to keep your home from becoming a dangerous place to live, but also to show existing homeowners how to keep their home safe for their families.

Many times, I've asked families how they would feel if something happened to a loved one that could have been prevented. I personally know I would never forgive myself if I didn't take the time to learn how to make my family and friends safe.

Understanding how a house works is becoming a lost art. With so many new homes being purchased every day, it is important for new homeowners to know how their new house operates, and about the functions that are designed to keep them safe. A few categories in this book may overlap, but this will emphasize how important they all are.

1

PURPOSE OF A REAL ESTATE AGENT

When searching for a real estate agent, finding an agent with experience will benefit you greatly. States require that real estate agents be licensed, and they are required to take classes in order to take the exam to get their real estate license (requirements vary state to state). They next need to work under a real estate broker for a specific period of time (again, requirements vary from state to state). Once that specific period of time is over, they can take another exam to become a real estate broker and open their own agency. During the time they are basically apprentices, the broker usually will take the time to educate their agents on other areas of real estate not taught during the real estate classes. Brokers can run their own agencies and decide how the commissions are shared and split between the agent and the broker. Both agents and brokers then need to take certain continuing education courses every one to two years in order to maintain their licenses.

Agents and brokers work strictly on commission, and both can work as either the buyer's agent or the seller's agent. With all the options out there and with so many listing companies, 95 percent of the listing properties have either agents or brokers listing the home. I would highly suggest you do your homework to find an agent or broker that you have the highest confidence in, and of course trust. You can then work with that agent or broker to find a home and stay with them until the end of your search. These agents and brokers will be investing a lot of their time to help you, and please remember that these agents and brokers work strictly on commission. Of course, there are times when the buyers or sellers lose faith in their agent or broker, and the need to find another agent or broker is necessary.

This book is also a great reference for real estate agents and brokers. Experienced agents and brokers usually join the buyer during the inspection by the home inspector. By doing this, over time, both agents and brokers become more knowledgeable on the condition of the home and any possible deficiencies. An agent having all this knowledge and a buyer having all this knowledge together would make a great team when looking for a home.

When searching for a new house for your family, your real estate agent or broker is responsible for showing you the houses that interest you. They also work with you to have the proper inspections done after the Purchase and Sale Agreement (P&S) has been signed. The due diligence segment of the P&S is typically restricted to 7-10 days depending on what is agreed to. After the due diligence period and all the inspections are done, then the negotiations begin regarding what the inspectors found and what needs to be corrected prior to the sale of the home.

2

PURPOSE OF A HOME INSPECTOR

The current owners (sellers) will need to fill out a form called the "Seller's Disclosures." This form informs the buyer of what will be left in the home after the sale, along with the types of heating system, HVAC systems, wastewater disposal, all appliances, roof condition and age. There can be many other things to list, but why I mention this is a lot of sellers check off the "unknown" box. Most times the owners are sincere about the information that they share, but there are times when they just do not want to disclose anything that may get the buyer to walk away from the sale.

As a certified home inspector, we always request the Seller's Disclosure so that we can determine the accuracy of the seller's information. I have caught a few discrepancies so, if you should have any questions, you should ask your home inspector to investigate it.

Wouldn't it be important to you to know what these items are prior to signing the P&S? Think about it: having all the inspections done, having to work on the negotiations to correct the deficiencies and then possibly losing the opportunity to purchase the home or possibly losing your deposit.

Not all banks, finance companies, and private lenders require a home inspection, but take my advice and get a home inspection done, even if it is not required. Even though a home inspector cannot see through walls, they are trained to look for mistakes made by homeowners doing their own renovations. Homeowners usually do renovations prior to listing their homes on the market and may not hire licensed and insured contractors. If your real estate agent suggests that you do not get a home inspection, they may be working with the seller's agent to cover up a problem with the home that they know a home inspector would find and blow up the deal!

The home inspector is also there to give you a report on the condition of the home and any defects they discover during the inspection. The home inspector can only report what they can physically see, and not what is going on inside the walls. Every home inspector has a different way of inspecting the home, and every home inspector has a different way of preparing the report for the future homeowners. I have personally seen some inspectors in action and was very impressed with their inspections and reports. On the other hand, I have heard reports from some real estate agents and brokers about those bad inspectors who rush through the inspection and miss so many deficiencies. Also, there are those inspectors who blow the deal because they make a big deal out of some minor deficiencies. I have done many inspections for both myself and my clients, and I always explain how these situations can be corrected and an approximate cost to correct them.

With all due respect to real estate agents and brokers, they are trained to work with you to help you locate the house that suits you and your family. A truly seasoned real estate professional may recognize most of the deficiencies even before you hire a home inspector, but I have seen many issues missed by both real estate agents and inspectors. So, the more you know, the easier it is to catch these issues and address them before you even enter into a purchase and sale agreement or hire an inspector. This also avoids having to deal with negotiations with the present owner.

3

NEIGHBORHOOD AND HOME LOCATION

1. Which Side of the Street?

Location of your home is one of the many considerations you need to address (no pun intended). Whether you have a young family or older family, having the sidewalk on your side of the street could either be an asset or a liability.

For instance, young children learning to ride a bike or skateboarding are much safer on the sidewalk than in the street.

Knowing which direction your future home is facing (north, south, east, or west) should also be a factor when considering buying your future home.

If the home has a southern exposure, because the sun rises in the east and sets in the west, the front of your home will always have direct sunlight, and that sunlight may be limited in your backyard. Having direct sunlight also means that damaging UV rays are now deteriorating your windows, doors, siding and trim. Also, the paint will fade faster, and depending on the type of siding on the home, will even cause vinyl siding to fade.

If the home has a northern exposure, just the opposite will happen with the sunlight. It should be something to consider if you have future plans for the backyard (pools, spas, gazebos, playground sets, etc.).

2. Position on the Street

Having your new home located on the corner of two streets may make it more difficult to enter and exit your driveway. Cars stopping at stop signs will make you have to wait to get in or out of your driveway. Also, it is more dangerous for a family of small children. Privacy is also more difficult with houses on all four sides of your home. Fences can solve that problem, but you must figure in the added expense if you plan to move forward and buy the house.

Having your new home located further away from an intersection will allow easier access to your home's driveway. Also, it is much safer for children to stay away from intersections.

If the home you're considering is at the end of a dead-end road or on a cul-de-sac, you need to prepare yourselves for intrusive headlights. During the nighttime hours, your neighbors' and/or their guests' headlights will be shining right into your home's front windows. Depending on the bedroom locations, the lights from those headlights could be very annoying.

In older neighborhoods, a dead-end road meant that the road just ends with no place to turn around without pulling into a neighbor's driveway. This type of dead-end road makes it very difficult for delivery trucks, trash pickup, and your family and friends when visiting. Also, if you have school-age children, be aware that school buses are unable to go down the street since there is no way to turn around. Your children would have to wait at the end of the street to ride the bus.

My biggest concern about a dead-end road is that emergency vehicles are now limited and may even have to back down the road to get to an emergency. The extra time needed to do this now takes away precious time to get to that emergency.

If you have a young family, dead-end roads can give you more peace of mind from road traffic and additional safe space for your children to ride their bikes. Alternatively, if you have an elder living with you, this could be more of an issue if EMS must be called in for assistance. Please keep all this in mind when looking for your home.

My former sister-in-law wanted to purchase a house at the end of a long shared street with another home. My ex-father-in-law asked the real estate agent is the street was a town approved road, and the agent stated that it was. Shortly after the sale was the first snow storm, and the street was never plowed. I called the town DPW to ask why, and I was informed that the road was not a town approved road. It took some time and a few phone calls to get this approved, so please make sure you do your due diligence.

3. Neighborhood Houses

Viewing your possible neighborhood's houses should be considered. How old is the development and how do your future neighbors take care of their homes and landscaping? What type of vehicles do they drive, and do they keep them maintained and cared for? All of which should help you determine your comfort level for you and your family.

I remember getting some advice when I was looking for my first home. I was told that you should visit the neighborhood of the house you're interested in a few times at different times of the day. This will help you determine the local traffic, walkers and bikers, and general activity in the neighborhood.

The one thing I neglected to do at the time, because I was so excited to buy this home, was to check out the neighborhood. I did not notice until after I moved in that there was a large apartment complex located at the top of the street. My house was located on the corner of two streets, and it was a major roadway for all the tenants to come and go to their apartments. They also were in the habit of driving over my lawn to make the turn. I had to place large rocks around that corner to keep them from driving on my lawn.

4. Emergency Services

If you're not originally from the area that you're looking to reside in, you also may want to locate the nearest fire and police departments, as well as the local hospital.

I had a nice cabin cruiser back in the '90s that was kept at a marina on Cape Cod. My children were both under 10 and my youngest decided to stand up on a chair. He fell backwards and had a gash on the back of his head because he landed on the back of an opened metal door. I had to ask a fellow boater if they knew where the nearest hospital was. In hindsight, as a responsible parent, I should have known where it was in the first place. Ever since then, I always check where these services are whenever we travel anywhere.

If you have a young family, even teenagers, accidents do happen, and medical assistance may be necessary. Children fall off bikes, scooters, and skateboards; bones break, along with various cuts and scrapes. Not only is knowing where the medical services are located important for children, it is equally important for us adults and our parents and visitors.

My father and stepmother were visiting one summer afternoon and my father was inside the house taking a nap while the rest of us were outside enjoying the warm weather and pool time. My father, who usually joined us in the pool, was fast asleep in the living room. I asked my stepmother if he had been doing this a lot and she said that he had been napping a lot lately.

Knowing this is not normal activity for my dad, I went in and woke him up to talk with him. Having many years of first aid, CPR, and first responder training, the flags were all raising inside my head. I suggested to him that since the fire station was right down the street, we should go and get his blood pressure and pulse checked. Of course, his response was, "I'm not going down to the fire station to have them check me out." My response to him was, "Dad, we can do this the easy way or the hard way. In other words, either we can go to them, or I'll have them come to us." He finally agreed and I got him in the car and drove straight to the fire station. I went in and asked one of the paramedics to come out to take his vitals. They gladly and quickly came out and discovered that his blood pressure and pulse were extremely low. I asked them what they would suggest, and their answer was to get him to the hospital as quickly as possible.

I looked at my father again and said, "Dad, I'm taking you to the hospital." Once again, his response was, "I'm not going to the hospital." My response once again was, "Dad, we can do this the easy way or the hard way but either way we're going." After a few more grumbles, he finally agreed.

To make a long story short, it ended up that my father had v-fib and they needed to insert a pacemaker. Why I share this story is that these situations happen and knowing what to do and where to go may be a matter of life or death.

If you are at the age to be able to purchase a home or condo, I'm sure you've interacted with at least one of these services.

Where we live, a fire station is less than a mile away. We also live off a very busy street with a lot of car traffic, trucks, and buses that you can drown out after a while, but when the fire trucks and ambulances go by, they must sound their horns and sirens as they get near the intersection. These sirens are around 110-120 decibels and can cause hearing damage with even less than one minute of exposure. An airplane's engine noise averages around 150 decibels and fireworks average around 150-175 decibels.

When you're looking to purchase a home or condo, remember that the types of emergency services available vary depending on what the city or town it's in will offer. It is common knowledge that your tax dollars pay for all these services, so the smaller the community, the smaller the services that are offered to its citizens. Obviously the bigger the city, the higher the budget for police, fire, and emergency medical services.

Without getting into specifics, both police and fire departments are given specific budgets to fund and administer their departments. Larger departments can split up responsibilities between police officers and firefighters. Smaller departments do not have that luxury and need to unload more responsibilities on each officer or firefighter. This also affects their ability to have more specialized training or even be able to take the time to do so.

In my hometown, one of my former classmates is the police chief, and another one of my former officers is the fire chief. I know of the struggles they have every year to keep their budgets funded and make sure their officers and firefighters have continual access to proper training. Finding that balance is very stressful for both chiefs.

If either one of these departments is in a city or suburban area, usually the entire area uses city water. If city water is available, fire trucks can refill their pumpers using fire hydrants to fight the fires. If you're located in a more rural area and you have your own water well, fire trucks have no way to refill their pumpers unless the fire is near a lake or stream. In that case, in most areas, the fire department may need to use your well or even multiple wells to put out the fire.

My ex-father-in-law built a house in a very rural area back in the 1980s and needed to have a well installed for the home. He was told by the installer that by current town law, he was responsible to report to the local authorities if this well could pump so many gallons per minute in case of a local fire.

When the home was built may help determine when or if the home's well is on that list. Just keep this in mind when you're looking at a home in a rural area; it may be your home or your neighbor's home that may depend on that well water to save their home in case of a fire.

No matter where your future home may be located, there are always potential dangers in your area. Gas, water, and sewer lines running by your future home are susceptible to leakage depending on when they were installed. I have seen firsthand the erosion damage done to a street when a water main breaks and floods the street. Older natural gas lines also can leak and cause explosions that may even affect your home.

When I owned my daycare center, a man from the local gas company knocked on the door and wanted to check for any gas leaks in the building. I told him that the prior owner used to have natural gas, but we converted the system to oil and abandoned the gas line which was shut off at the street. He told me that even though the gas line was shut off at the street that, if there was a gas leak, any lines around that pipe could follow the pipe back into the building.

So, if you have someone knocking at your door, make sure they have the proper credentials and let them test for a gas leak.

The lifespan of your natural gas meter is anywhere from 10-25 years depending on the model installed on or in your home. Your local gas provider should be sending you a notice when your meter needs to be replaced. If you have any questions regarding your meter, contact your local gas provider.

Let's review some potential dangers surrounding your future home. Knowing what is going on around you will keep you and your family safe.

5. *Trains*

When doing your research for a new home, knowing if there is a train track in the area is important. Trains not only transport passengers, they also transport freight, fuel, and all types of dangerous chemicals.

It is the responsibility of your local authorities to know what travels over those tracks in case of a derailment. Whatever chemicals are being transported will determine the evacuation radius needed to protect those living and working in that evacuation zone.

Where we live there are freight trains that toot their airhorns at all times of the day and night. Train air horns blast at approximately 96 decibels (average smoke detectors are approximately 85 decibels) and can be heard anywhere from four to five miles away.

The recommended distance to reside or work away from a train track is approximately 500-1,000 feet in case of train cars derailing. Train vibrations can even be felt up to a mile away.

When doing a construction inspection in Boston, Massachusetts, I was on the second floor when the local commuter train went by. This building has parking under the building on the ground level, offices on the second floor, and condos on the third through fifth floors. Unfortunately, the new owners will have to live with the train's air horns and the vibration of the train running over the rails. The back of the building was built with extra insulation and soundproof windows, but the vibration is still being felt.

6. Airports & Airplanes

If the house or condo you're looking for is located near an airport, your future home may be in or near the airport's flight paths for takeoffs and landings. Just how close you are will determine how low the planes are, and how loud the roar of the engines will be.

A house I renovated in Warwick, Rhode Island is located a few miles from the airport and in one of the flight paths. When the planes fly overhead the engine noise is so loud you must stop whatever conversation you're having and wait for the plane to fly by.

Even though your future home may be further away, you're taking a risk that the airport may need to be expanded. This was the case at the T.F. Green Airport in Warwick. Many houses were bought by the airport on or near the future runways, and many families were given money to purchase windows and other forms of noise reducing improvements for their homes.

Either way, the value of the homes located in these areas dropped and some were even leveled to make room for the new runways. Just more to consider if you want to move you and your family to these areas.

7. *Industrial & Manufacturing Zones*

Buying a home or condo near industrial or manufacturing zones could be very concerning. Again, your local EMS is also responsible for knowing what chemicals are used in these industrial and manufacturing buildings.

Our auxiliary police department trained every month during our monthly meetings. Many of these training sessions involved our fire department and firefighters. They shared a story of a police officer who was chasing a suspect through a chemical plant and accidentally brushed up against a box full of toxic chemicals. They caught the suspect and then after his shift, he went home and got a big hug around his leg from his five-year-old son. The son went to bed that night and never woke up the next morning.

This, along with many other reasons, is why cities and towns mandate that any business that uses or stores any dangerous chemicals report this to their local EMS. If something happens in those buildings, EMS wants to ensure that their officers and firefighters are protected and safe during an emergency.

NEIGHBORHOOD AND HOME LOCATION *19*

8. Group Homes—Shelters—Methadone Clinics & Nursing Homes

All these types of homes and businesses are an asset for those people who need them. If you decide to purchase a home within walking distance of any of these places, just keep in mind what may happen.

A friend of mine owns an auto service station on a main street where we live. He told me about this methadone clinic that had just opened next door to his building. He said now he has so many people walking past his facility and hanging out around his building while waiting for their appointments.

You should do your homework and find out if there are any group homes in the area and what their purpose is. Is it a halfway home to help reformed convicts, drug or alcohol addiction, people with mental disorders, or a shelter for battered women?

Be aware that these homes and shelters are not usually advertised for the health and safely of the occupants. They are also usually manned 24/7/365 with staff trained to handle the clients they care for. Sometimes those clients step out of line and local police are called in to handle the offender. These offenses usually don't happen during the day, so if you're looking for your future home near one of these facilities, you may be woken up with lights and sirens.

Nursing homes are necessary to care for our elders and mentally challenged people. They deal with both medical and mental illnesses, including dementia. Usually, these facilities are designed to contain these patients, but they do escape and wander off. If your new home is near one of these facilities, you may have a visitor any time of the day or night, or a knock on the door asking if you've seen this person.

Just be cautious and vigilant about the security of your home and the protection of you and your family.

9. *Sex Offender Registry*

It is not the seller or agent's responsibility to inform you of any sex offenders that live in or near the neighborhood of the home you're interested in. You can contact the local police department for more information on the location of any sex offenders in the area. Also, you can perform a search on the national sex offender website to see who may be living in the area. I was able to do this and it's very eye-opening to see how many are living in our area.

4

TYPES OF HOMES

I don't remember anyone sitting down with me and explaining how this part of my life was going to proceed, so I had to discover this entirely on my own. As always, everyone's situations may differ, but this is the usual progression of a person's life.

When a person decides to leave their family home and go out into the world, they usually start with an apartment (either by themselves or with a friend or loved one). Then, as time progresses, maybe children arrive, and you've outgrown the existing apartment. Now you'll need to either move into a larger apartment or condo rental. Children do get older, and your family now needs an even larger space, so now you're looking for your home. Your financial position will determine whether you buy a larger condo, ranch, split-level (also known as a raised ranch), gambrel, colonial, or even a contemporary style home.

Now the time comes when you realize that you want to be a homeowner, and with that comes a whole new set of responsibilities. Those responsibilities include having to take care of the mortgage, insurance, real estate taxes, all maintenance and repairs, and, most of all, the security for your home and family.

Every homeowner I've spoken with, I tell them that their home is a living and breathing organism. The average home is built out of wood from trees milled down to various sizes used to build a house. The process of drying out the wood is called "kiln drying," which removes the moisture down to a specific target (usually around six percent). The wood is structured into a frame to support the design of the house and weight of the roof structure. That same wood is then encapsulated by insulation and either sheetrock or plaster, and then painted. The outside covering is some type of sheathing, and either shingles or siding is installed over that.

What I try to explain to homeowners is that wood is still a natural product which is still able to absorb and release moisture. During the winter months when the home's heating system is running, the air in the home becomes much drier and dries out the moisture content of not only the framed walls, but also any woodwork inside the home. That's when windows and doors may not open or close as well as they used to. Cracks may also form on walls, especially at stress points located in corners, ceilings, and over door and window headers.

Conversely, when the summer heat and humidity levels increase, that same wood inside the walls and interior wood will now absorb that moisture. This will cause the same areas to expand and cause the same effects as the heated air during the wintertime.

Depending on the age of the home, homeowners may hear wood cracking noises during the two extreme seasons. This is usually due to the expansion and contraction of all the wood inside the framing structure. My house is approximately 14 years old, and my wife and I still hear this noise coming from our attic during these extreme seasons of weather.

If you're going to purchase a home made completely of brick or block, you won't have as much going on inside the walls unless the inside framing is done with wood.

Condo living has its benefits and its downsides. If you're renting a condo, your landlord is responsible for the maintenance and upkeep of the property. If you're considering purchasing a condo, you're not responsible for the exterior maintenance and upkeep, but you now have to pay a fee to a homeowners' association (HOA) which pays subcontractors to maintain the property.

My son is a real estate broker and is representing a friend of his who is trying to sell her condo. Her reason for wanting to sell the condo is because of the exorbitant condo fee. Her condo association did not plan accordingly for future capital expenses such as a new roof. Because the condo association did not have enough funding, a surcharge was given equally to each condo owner in the association to make up the difference.

Most condos are built within close proximity of each other, either in groupings or on multiple floors. There are other types of complexes that have individual homes located on a shared piece of land. In this case, you're basically paying a fee to live in your home on that land and now you have to pay an HOA fee for all of the maintenance for the outside area. Again, HOAs should also have part of the fees put in escrow for upcoming major expenses.

A few months prior to this book being written, a large condo complex called Champlain Towers in Miami partially collapsed. My initial thought was that it might have been caused by a sinkhole, which Florida is known for. The building was inspected back in 2018 at which time several deficiencies in the below-grade parking lot were detected, including erosion in the building supports. The repairs were never done but the condo owners were each assessed a surcharge of $108,000. Because of the delay in getting the repairs done, 106 people died and several hundred lost their home.

So, if a condo interests you, whether in a small or large complex, make sure you confirm that the homeowners' association is well-funded and managed before you make any commitments.

If you're considering purchasing a ranch style home, knowing if the home has a full basement or is built on a slab makes a huge difference, not only in available space for possible storage or future renovation into an extra room, but maintenance wise. All the utilities usually run through the basement and are easily accessible in case of any leaks or other maintenance issues. With a home that has a slab foundation, there is no basement.

The electrical is usually done from the attic and wired down to the outlets, switches, lighting, and other fixtures and appliances, while the plumbing is installed in the cement floor. If any issues regarding plumbing surface, the home's floor would possibly have to be jack-hammered up to access the plumbing. This would be a very expensive undertaking and should be considered as a possible upcoming maintenance issue, especially if the home is older and plumbing has aged significantly.

With raised ranches, gambrels, and contemporary homes, again the plumbing is usually located in the ceiling of the basement and plumbed up to the different floors in the home. In older homes, the plumbing is usually copper pipes. In new homes, flexible tubing has replaced copper tubing due to the lower cost of the flexible tubing and the ease of running the tubing throughout the home.

As with anything new that comes out on the market, no long-term testing has been done. Plumbers are now going to newer homes to fix or replace the flexible tubing and the connectors for both hot and cold water. Cheap knockoffs were manufactured and used by some plumbers who wanted to save money on the job. This now results in the cheap knockoffs failing and causing flooding in homes. I am sharing this with you because I have experienced this myself.

With any home that has a basement that you're considering renovating in the future, I would highly suggest installing a dropped ceiling (ceiling grids and inserts). I have seen many homes that have had plumbing leaks and the homeowners were unable to locate the leak because they decided to sheetrock and plaster the ceilings. Water rarely flows directly down from where the leak begins. The water follows the ceiling to the lowest point and either causes a bubble in the ceiling that will eventually burst and flood the area, or it will find the nearest ceiling fixture and begin pouring out of the fixture which then causes an electrical problem. Now a plumber must come in and cut out large portions of the ceiling just to locate the leak. This project now becomes very messy and very expensive.

The type and style of home you're considering will determine where the bedrooms are located. Depending on your family's current or even future needs, how to get everyone out of the house in case of an emergency must be considered. More of this will be covered later in the book with other information on how to help keep your family safe, because having this knowledge is so important in choosing your future home.

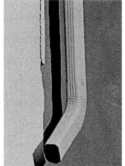

5

LANDSCAPING AND PROPER DRAINAGE

One of the many features of a well-built and designed home is the ability of the home to be able to shed any water off and away from itself.

The landscaping of your future home is very valuable information. Make sure that the slope of the land is going away from the home as that will keep the home dry during severe weather. Proper gutters and downspouts should also be pointing away from the home to allow the runoff from the roof not to puddle around the home. Not having proper landscaping and water runoff will cause flooding in the basement and cause extreme damage.

One of my clients had me inspect a home she was considering purchasing. It was a small two-story home approximately 1,300 square feet with a partially finished basement. I usually start my inspections in the basement and work my way up to the upper levels, ending in the attic. While inspecting the basement, I noticed one entire side of the basement wall was flaking and discolored. I felt the wall and it seemed to be very cold and moist. I used my moisture meter and measured the wall above the soil line. The moisture level was approximately 27 percent, which is acceptable. When I placed the moisture meter below the soil line, the moisture reading jumped up to 99.9 percent. I inspected the entire wall and got the same readings. We went outside and inspected the landscaping on that side of the home (which was blocked by a fence) and discovered that the ground level was completely flat with no pitch away from the home, and didn't allow for proper drainage of rainwater.

I advised the client that, for this to be corrected, the lawn would have to be excavated along the entire length of the wall and down to the footings. This wall would need time to dry out—anywhere from three to six months—and then be treated with a water barrier. The hole would have to be backfilled and the lawn sloped away from the foundation. Additionally, installing a French drain by the footings would be advisable. I estimated the cost would be at approximately $20,000 to $30,000.

With that and a few other major problems found, the client walked away and thanked me for the thorough inspection.

Another client in Newport, Rhode Island had just purchased a home and wanted an alarm system installed in the home. He wanted to make sure that we installed a water sensor near his back door. This sparked my curiosity, so I asked him why he needed a water sensor by the back door. He said that every time there was a heavy rainstorm, water would pool up in front of the door and slowly leak in over the threshold.

I looked outside and noticed that his gutters were not pitched correctly towards the downspouts. I suggested he get a gutter installer to come and correct the situation by changing the pitch and the flooding would then stop.

Another thing to look for regarding flooding potential is any water stains on the basement wall. These stains represent a flood that occurred in the basement and the stain will tell you how high the floodwater was. The only ways to cover the stain are to paint the unfinished wall or renovate the basement. Keep in mind, this stain could have occurred from groundwater rising through the basement or walls, or due to plumbing problems such as a broken water main or leaky hot water tank.

Trees should also be considered when you're looking at a new home. Large trees that overhang the roof can cause damage to the shingles and even the roof decking. As a rule, trees should not be close enough to a home that if they fall, damage would be done to the house. Many trees get uprooted during severe weather and end up falling on homes and creating a very dangerous situation for the occupants.

Everyone likes to have plantings around the home, but a frequent mistake they make is planting shrubs that eventually grow against the house and do damage to the siding. Maintaining proper pruning is very important, and high shrubbery also gives potential burglars a place to hide, but I'll cover this later on in the book.

In March and April of 2010, the northeast was hit with a variety of rainstorms that was termed the "100-year flood." Many communities had anywhere from 10 to 16 inches of water. All local rivers crested over the riverbanks; local roads were flooded, and some washed away. Mall parking lots had over two feet of water and entire communities were underwater.

I share this information with you because my philosophy is that it isn't advisable to purchase a home in an area prone to possible flooding. I currently own a home with my wife, and we live right across the street from one of the city's water towers. I feel comfortable enough that if something ever happens to that huge tank, the water has a path to flow without washing our home away and off the foundation.

Knowing this information should help you understand that, if you go through with the sale, you can forecast what you need to do to make your new home safe.

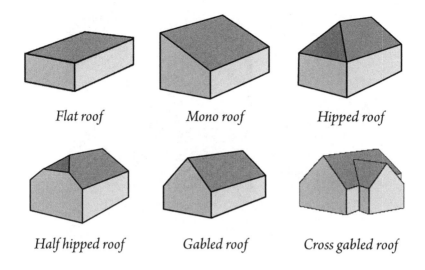

Flat roof   Mono roof   Hipped roof

Half hipped roof   Gabled roof   Cross gabled roof

6

STRUCTURAL

1. Roof Structures

The picture shown above exhibits the basic styles of roof structures. There is no such thing as a good or bad roof structure; it is all based on the aesthetics of the home and/or possibly the neighborhood. Just be aware that when the time comes to replace the roof covering, the bigger the roof, the higher the cost. Hipped roofs are usually more expensive because of the material waste to cover the angled design.

The various roof designs also determine whether there is any available storage space inside the attic. Gable roofs usually offer the most available storage space. Also, the higher the pitch of the roof, the more height available inside the attic space.

2. Roof Ventilation & Insulation

The sun heats up the roof's surface, and that heat flows through the roof deck and into the attic space. The picture above shows insulation baffles that allows the flow of air from the soffits up to the ridge vent.

Adequate ventilation and insulation inside the home's attic is very important and controls the temperature inside the home. If the attic is not properly vented, heat builds up in the attic and slowly works its way down into the home. In other words: the hotter the attic, the hotter the home.

There are many different types of attic vents to vent the roof; some even work using electricity, also known as a power vent.

I have seen the inside of hundreds of attics, and I have seen the results of improper ventilation. Mold and moisture build up inside the attics and then become a health issue.

When insulating a home, the only area that needs to be insulated is the actual living space of the home. I had one client that thought it would be a good idea to insulate the roof rafters inside of his attic area. Then, to top that off, he decided to put a plastic vapor barrier over the insulation. I tried to educate him on why this was

not a good idea because your attic needs to breathe. Just to demonstrate, I brushed my hand over the plastic and my hand was covered with moisture. Needless to say, this demonstration changed his mind and he said he was going to remove both the insulation and the plastic vapor barrier.

Another reason for not insulating the roof rafters is because you're now trapping the heat from the sun coming through the shingles and the roof deck. Now the shingles are being cooked from the outside and the inside. This reduces the life of the shingles and may possibly void the warranty.

3. Roof Coverings

As with all other sections, this section is designed to provide a short overview for the reader without getting into any details about types of installations for each of these types of roofing materials.

ASPHALT SHINGLES

There are many different types and styles of roof coverings. The most popular are asphalt shingles and the life expectancy ranges

anywhere from 15 to 30 years depending on the manufacturer. Do not be fooled by a "lifetime transferable warranty" that may come with the house you're looking at. First of all, the manufacturer knows that the average family moves anywhere from 7 to 10 years, and they hope that the homeowners have either lost the documents or completely forgotten about the warranty. Even if the current homeowners state that they have the documents, the fine print will tell you that they are only liable to replace the shingles and are not responsible for stripping off the old roof and installing the replacement shingles.

Your home inspector must rely on their own knowledge and experience regarding the condition of the shingles. Regarding the actual age of the shingles, they must rely on the seller's disclosure forms.

Asphalt singles weigh an average of 400-450 pounds per square (1 square = 10-by-10-foot area). The picture shown above is a roof with two layers of shingles.

If you're looking at a home and the homeowners tell you that they just replaced the roof, make sure to find out if they covered over the existing roof with newer shingles. The reason why they do this is because, in most jurisdictions, they are allowed to do so, and it's anywhere from 50 to 75 percent cheaper than the cost of a full roof replacement. By doing so they could be covering up potential problems that even a home inspector can't see or report on. Putting a second layer on the home reduces the life of the shingle by almost half its lifespan and will void any manufacturer's warranty.

Also, the weight of another layer of shingles puts a lot of stress on the roof structure and walls. I've seen roofs sagging and even walls cracking because of the weight and stress on the home.

Just keep all this in mind when looking at a home and if you're considering purchasing it. You may be replacing the roof sooner than you expected.

FLAT ROOFING SYSTEMS

Depending on what type of home you're looking at, it may have a full or partially flat roof. The type of roofing is a rubber membrane with an average lifespan of 20 to 30 years if it is installed correctly. The purpose of installing a rubber membrane is because the pitch is too low for asphalt shingles. The minimum pitch for asphalt roofs is 2:12, which means that the height of the roof only increases two inches in height every 12 inches across.

METAL ROOF SYSTEMS

Metal roofing dates back into the 1700s but has come a long way since then. Metal systems were usually about two to three times the cost of asphalt shingles, but the new metal systems last two to four times longer than an asphalt shingled roof.

Metal roofing is gaining momentum because the cost of the material and installation costs are coming down. These new styles are very aesthetically pleasing and come in all shapes and colors.

The picture above shows "snow guards" that should be placed on metal roofs for protection. Snow and ice melt faster on metal roofs, and any large accumulations of snow or ice become very dangerous when they slide off the roof. On average, about 15 people die each year from falling snow or ice. Having snow guards slows down the melting process and keeps large sections of snow or ice from sliding off. It is also good to know these snow guards will protect your landscaping shrubs and flowers.

TERRACOTTA ROOF SYSTEMS

Terracotta, clay, and cement roofing tiles cost approximately three to four times as much as asphalt shingles. These materials can last for centuries and some even come with a 50-year warranty. The

weight of these tiles can be as much as 600-650 pounds per square (1 square = 10-by-10-foot area).

If you're considering purchasing a home and renovating it to include terracotta or any other clay or cement roof system, I would highly suggest that you hire a structural engineer to make sure the roof structure can handle the additional weight.

SLATE ROOF SYSTEMS

Slate roofs are beautiful, and you'll find them mostly on very expensive homes and mansions. They come in a wide variety of colors that really bring out the beauty of the roof design and home.

Slate roofing systems weigh anywhere from 800-1,500 pounds per square (1 square = a 10-by-10-foot area) depending on the thickness of the slate you're installing. Soft slate can last anywhere from 50 to 100 years, and hard slate can last 75 to 200 years. The cost of this type of roofing system can be as much five to seven times the cost of asphalt shingles, not to mention that just finding a company to install them is like finding a needle in a haystack.

If you're considering purchasing a home with a slate roof, keep in mind how much money you'll need to have in reserve to replace this very expensive feature.

SOLAR PANELS

This is just an overview of having solar panels installed on a residential roof. There are many companies offering various purchase and leasing plans, so do your research before buying a home with these panels or if you're looking to have solar panels installed after you purchase the home.

Most solar panel companies require that the solar panels be installed on a new roof. The reasoning is that the solar panels are designed to last for 25 years, and the installation cost is factored into the initial installation. They do not want to incur the cost (nor do you!) if the asphalt roofing shingles need to be replaced within that 25-year period.

Metal roofs, terracotta roofs, and slate roofs can also have solar panels installed with a different type of bracketing. Installation companies list a wide variety of requirements, so please do your homework ahead of time.

4. Roof Condition

Roofs are what protect your home, family, and possessions against all types of weather. The most traditional roof is asphalt shingles.

I had a client in northern Massachusetts that had just installed their dream kitchen. They paid over $30,000 for this gorgeous custom kitchen. The roof leaked during a very bad storm and destroyed a third of the brand new kitchen cabinets. I asked them if they knew the roof was leaking and they responded with, "Yes, but we didn't know how bad."

I always inform everyone I know who is looking to purchase a home or renovate it that when you build a home, you start from the foundation up, but when you're renovating a home, you start from the roof and work your way down. The roof protects you, your family, and everything you own from all types of weather. Take care of your roof and it will continue to do its job. If you neglect it, the damage will be very expensive and aggravating.

SAGGING ROOF

Whenever I arrive at a home for an inspection, the first thing I see is the condition of the roof and the shingles.

One of my clients was a disabled veteran who just purchased his home a few months ago. It was a small three-bedroom ranch located in a rural area, and on a small lot.

When I arrived, I noticed that the roof's ridgeline was dipping in the middle. This sent up a red flag immediately, and I knew something was structurally wrong. I took out my binoculars and began examining the roof and realized that the roof had three layers of shingles on it.

After I met the new owner, we sat down and he told me about his new home. I asked him if he had a home inspection prior to purchasing the house, and his response was, "In order to get the loan to purchase the house I had to have a home inspection done." I then informed him that while I was outside, I discovered that he had three layers on the roof and that the weight was making the roofline sag. I asked him if I could look in the attic to see if any damage was done. After looking in the attic, I discovered that all the collar ties that keep the roofing frame together had snapped in half due to the weight of the roof and the three layers of shingles.

Triangles are the strongest design for construction. The purpose of the collar ties is to prevent the roof rafters from spreading apart due to roof coverings and snowloads, and affecting the home's ridgeline.

The disturbing part of this story is that the home inspector never caught or disclosed this to the new owner. In turn, he didn't disclose that the roof was collapsing and could collapse on top of him. After showing the vet the condition of the roof, he agreed to let us fix it. Due to the severity of the situation, I asked him if he had a place to stay until we got the roof done.

Another time I was asked to inspect a home for a couple that wanted to buy the house they lived in, which was owned by a family member. During my inspection, I noticed that the family owners removed the garage door and renovated the garage for more living space. I noticed that the ceiling was sagging in this room and went outside to view the roof over the old garage. I discovered that when the room was renovated, they took out the center supports for the ceiling joists. Removing the supports caused the garage roof to sag, along with the ceiling in the room. This created a potential hazard because the weight of the roof was not supported properly, and probably was not even able to handle the snow loads here in the northeast.

If the house you're looking at needs a new roof, make sure you find a reliable and trustworthy roofer. Also make sure that the roofer uses a service that measures the roof via satellite. One I'm familiar with is Eagle View. Make sure you get a copy of the report that verifies the amount of shingles you need. This keeps the contractor honest, and from quoting a much higher price to replace the roof.

There are many videos available that show the proper way to re-shingle a roof. If you need to get a new roof, I highly advise that you view some videos and have your contractor explain exactly what the process is that they will perform. There are basically three types of construction companies: the GOOD, the BAD, and the UGLY. I've seen and inspected faulty roofs from all three categories.

5. Balloon vs. Conventional Construction

The age of the home will determine what type of framing it was built with. In older homes, usually from the 1860s to the 1940s, the homes were built with balloon framing. With this type of framing, all the sides of the home are built first; then floors are added and attached to the side walls of the exterior framing. The problem with this type of framing is that there is no fire blocking between the floors. This style of framing was changed because, if a fire were to start in the basement, it would be able to travel up through the walls and end up in the attic. The fire would then engulf the home up from the basement and down from the attic, trapping the home-owners inside.

New conventional framing now offers built-in fire blocking on each floor. The first floor is built directly on top of the foundation walls. The walls are then built on top of the floor joists, and the ceiling joists are added for the next floor and so forth.

I have also seen balloon framing vary with regards to spacing between the two-by-fours. I have seen the framing vary anywhere from 16 to 24 inches depending on who the contractor was that built the house. Building codes weren't very good back in those days, but the code has greatly improved, and enforcement must be done with building permits and signatures of inspectors.

Why should you be aware of this, and is balloon framing dangerous? Balloon framing was dangerous when homes were heated by coal or woodstoves. If the stove were to break open, coal or wood would become exposed to the wooden timbers of the home, and because of the constant heat drying out the wooden frame of the house, the conditions were perfect for a fire to start and spread quickly. With today's technology, heating systems are extremely safe with emergency shutoffs built in.

Again, I mean no disrespect to real estate agents, but just a little training on what to watch for structurally will save a lot of grief for their clients. Home inspectors have no excuse to have missed this big deficiency, but I've seen this too many times in my career.

7

SIDING

Siding on older homes could be cedar shingles, hardboard, cement, brick, or various types of veneer. Asbestos was also used for siding because of its ability to protect the home from nearby and approaching fires. It was later determined that asbestos was a hazardous material and it is no longer used for home siding. Asbestos is safe if it's not disturbed and can also be sided over with other materials such as vinyl or other veneers. If the house you're looking for has recently been sided over, you should ask what type of siding is under the new siding.

Vinyl siding has become the go-to siding for most homes these days because of the cost, ease of installation, and durability. There are many different types of vinyl siding, as well as different grades. I have personally seen entire sides of homes fade on the southern exposure side due to the sun's UV rays. Cheaper siding does not have enough UV protection added into the manufacturing process and will fade within a few years. Again, make sure you do your homework; ask questions about the type and grade of siding when purchasing your new home.

Many homeowners go through the process of upgrading and updating their home when they're thinking about selling. Be careful and make sure you ask before you sign that purchase and sales agreement!

8

ENTRY DOORS

There are so many types of entry doors available at home improvement stores. If the home you're looking for has the wrong type of door or it doesn't work properly, your home inspector will report this to you.

By code, any apartment, condo, or home must have at least two means of egress. The front entry door is usually cosmetically nice to look at but should be made of either metal or solid wood. If the home has an attached garage door, the door must be either metal or a fire-rated wooden door. To verify if the solid core wooden door is fire-rated, a metal tag stating the rating is located on the top or on the hinged side of the door.

A friend of mine asked me to do a home inspection for a house he was purchasing. The home had a three-car garage and the prior owner decided to renovate one bay of the garage and make it a bedroom. I'm sure the prior owner didn't know this (or maybe he did and didn't get proper permits because a licensed contractor would know better) but building codes do not allow an access door from a garage to a bedroom. This is not permitted due to the possibility that, if a car is in the garage with the engine running, the carbon monoxide can penetrate the bedroom. This building code also covers any open venting from the garage into the home.

Back in the early 1990s, I decided to purchase a foreclosed home on Cape Cod. The short story is that the mortgage company gave me permission to break into the home to check on the oil tank and make sure the heater was working. We wanted to make sure, since it was during the winter, that the pipes wouldn't freeze and cause a flood.

When I approached the front door, I gave it a gentle push and the entire door just fell apart and landed inside the house. The next-door neighbor came over, introduced himself and asked what I was doing there. I told him the whole story and showed him the front door. He said not to worry about it, because the local drug enforcement agency had kicked that door in many times! Imagine my surprise, and now I had to replace it!

If you're thinking about buying and renovating a foreclosed property, make sure you do your homework and due diligence prior to purchasing. Many people are looking for depressed and foreclosed properties to buy, renovate, and sell for a profit. They usually use the cheapest materials and cover up many existing problems with the home, so again, please do your homework and make sure proper permits were pulled, and still hire a home inspector.

9

WINDOWS

Two good friends of ours, Heather and Dave, asked about some windows they wanted replaced in their home. In our area of Massachusetts and Rhode Island, we have programs available through our local utility companies that aid in lowering our utility costs. They also offer financial assistance if the homeowners want to increase the insulation in the walls and attics, and this also includes replacing the windows in the home.

Back when I was growing up in the '60s and '70s, most homes only had single pane glass and the heat loss was incredibly high. Then, storm windows were developed, which we were able to add to the outside of the home to reduce that heat loss. Those windows attached to the home and had both storm windows and screens, so in the warmer weather the storm windows could be lifted, and the screen could be lowered to get more airflow through the house. The storm windows were usually unpainted and unprotected aluminum and would oxidize and look terrible over time.

In the mid-'70s the idea was created to have two panes of glass in the window, which would slow down the transfer of heat through the glass and windows, basically taking the place of the storm windows and looking much more appealing.

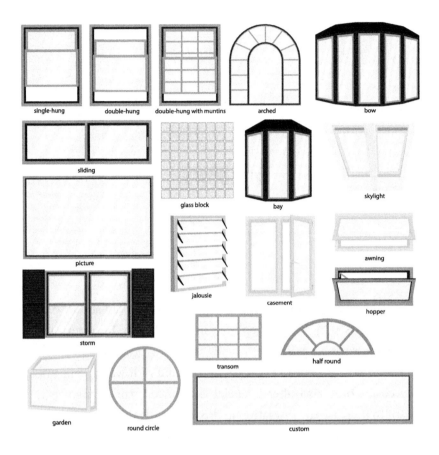

Later in the '70s and '80s further research was done to add argon gas between the two panes of glass. Argon gas is a very dense gas that is clear, odorless, and designed to slow down the heat loss (convection) from the windows.

As the low E glass (Low Emittance Glass) became more popular and less expensive over time, state and local building codes began requiring that only these windows be installed in both new and existing homes.

Along with argon gas, krypton gas was introduced, which has a better performance rating than argon, but was more expensive. As always, as time goes on, the cost of manufacturing was reduced, making these windows more available to the general public.

Statistics show that both argon and krypton gas will dissipate at the rate of approximately one percent per year and usually last anywhere from 15 to 20 years. Most manufacturers will offer a warranty for a specific period so that they can market their windows to perform better than other competitors. The manufacturers also know that the average family will move and purchase another home within 7 to 10 years, and that their transferable warranty information will get lost in the conveyance of the homes.

Also, most manufacturers will push the krypton gas along with triple pane glass. Don't fall for these practices, because the savings on heat or cooling loss will take 20 years to earn your money back.

As I stated earlier about the average progression of you and your family, investing in new windows should be thoroughly investigated and reviewed for the return on your investment.

If you're planning on staying in your home for an extended period of time, then you can justify the cost of the windows. I've moved 14 times, and I've said this almost every time I bought or built a new home.

When you go to a showing of a potential home you're looking at, take a few minutes to look at the windows and find out how old they are. If you see any cloudiness in the windows, that means that the gas has escaped the double pane and the window is no longer energy efficient. You may just want to keep this in mind if you're thinking of replacing the windows. Also, having financial assistance from your local utility company will make it very affordable, with immediate return on your investment.

There are two different ways to replace your windows: insert or full-frame. The difference is that with a replacement window, the installers take out the top and bottom sashes and insert another window inside that same opening. When this is done, the installation looks okay, but the window opening will now become smaller to accommodate the new window. This method is used quite frequently because the cost is much less and the return on your investment is much faster.

With a full-frame window, the entire window is removed, including the interior and exterior moldings. The window is then attached to the home with a nailing flange around the entire window. Insulation is then installed along with new caulking and window framing. Installations will vary with the type of siding your home has. Many videos are available online to show the various types of installations, and I would highly recommend viewing them.

There are many styles of windows available, but in a newer home the builders usually install construction grade vinyl windows (aka new construction windows). Prices may vary, but those windows are usually around $200 each, not installed.

Replacement window companies offer construction grade windows be inserted into the old frames, especially if the other windows are much older and the gas has dissipated. The windows are usually made from recycled plastics and have hollow frames that they claim will add to your home's fuel efficiency. Because these frames are hollow, the construction grade windows will eventually warp over time and are very hard to even open. If the windows are in direct sunlight every day, this condition will happen much faster than with those windows located in partially shaded areas of the home.

Manufacturers that offer full-frame windows will charge anywhere from $800 to $5,000 depending on the size and location of the windows. The windows are usually a solid core frame and will not warp as fast as the hollow frame windows.

Make sure you do your homework and research prior to making any decisions about replacing your windows. There are so many unscrupulous marketing and installation companies out there that will push you to make a quick decision and supposedly save you money. If they give you that type of pitch, just thank them for their time and ask them to please leave.

Here's a security tip: Window shades and curtains are not only for decoration. Keeping them open to allow sunlight into your home is important for our physical and mental health, but closing them at night is important for our safety. Burglars can easily see into your home if your lights are on and the shades and/or curtains are open.

Just an FYI, if the home you're looking to possibly purchase has bars on the windows, you might want to find out why. Are the current owners worried that burglars may try to come in through the window, or are they concerned that their 100-pound German shepherd may try to jump through? Just look around the neighborhood and see if anyone else has barred their windows. If you see many more homes with barred windows, it's more than likely that the neighbors are concerned about break-ins. If this is the case, you may want to reconsider your options!

10

OVERHEAD GARAGE DOORS

When you're shopping for your new home, having a garage is a big plus. Although their original design was a place to keep your vehicles protected from the weather, they're also there to allow you and your family to have access to the house without going outside in the elements.

The chance you'll find a garage which is actually used as a garage is very slim. I've inspected many homes where the garage is full of all types of junk: leftover appliances, broken down vehicles/bicycles/motorcycles, clothing, lawn equipment (usable and not usable) and old children's toys.

My point is that even if you added up the net worth of all those items, it won't come anywhere near the value of the vehicle that sits outside and gets exposed to the weather 24/7/365. Just a little knowledge to share when you're looking at the future value of your new garage.

Overhead garage doors come in many shapes and sizes. In older homes, the doors are usually just framed, non-insulated doors. They provide no insulation for the garage or home, but they do keep out the other elements: rain, snow, and wind.

There are so many options now for garage door replacements. Beautiful, detailed doors now come fully insulated and keep the home warmer in an attached garage. The only downside is that you should always park your car straight-in forward. Now that the garage is fully insulated, make sure that you open the garage door prior to starting and running your engine. Carbon monoxide will still build up quickly inside, so don't let your vehicle idle inside the garage for even a short period of time. If you want to warm up the vehicle in colder weather, a good practice is to back it out of the garage first.

 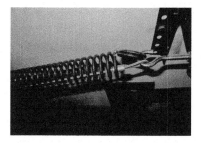

The purpose of the garage door springs is to counterbalance the weight of the door. When the garage door is closed, all the tension is now on the springs, to be ready to open the door with ease. This is when the springs are the most dangerous, and the safety cables are very valuable. Again, this is something that your home inspector would pick up on and explain to you, but having this knowledge ahead of time is also very valuable.

The usual types of spring that lift the door are either "extension springs" or "torsion springs." There are others available now that use chains and automatic lifts that can be controlled by your smartphone. Some alarm companies also offer garage door controls that can be controlled by your smartphone.

Extension springs are the most common, especially in older homes. When I bought my first home back in the mid-'80s, my garage had the extension springs. I came home one day after work to find the left extension spring in the middle of my driveway. It obviously snapped under the tension and went through the glass of the garage door and landed in the middle of the driveway. My first thought was, "I'm glad we weren't home when this happened because we would have been severely injured if any of us were near the garage."

I obviously replaced the broken spring and thought it would be a good idea to just replace them both as the other one might be next to snap. I'm glad I did this because the replacement springs come with a safety cable that goes inside the spring to protect the homeowners in case it snapped. If it did snap, the spring would bounce back and forth on the safety cable and eventually stop moving, and not cause any damage to anyone or the property.

Even though torsion springs have been around since the mid-1800s, they began being used in residential homes in the late 1990s to 2000s. They have a nicer appearance than the extension springs, and usually have an average life of 10,000 lifts (both up and down).

Living in my current home, my wife and I were sitting in the living room when we heard a loud bang from our garage. It sounded like someone just drove through the house. After jumping off the couch, we discovered that the left torsion spring had snapped (being under pressure because the garage door was closed). Since the springs counterbalanced the weight of the door, we were unable to even open the door manually.

I contacted the company that originally installed the opener and springs, and they did suggest that we replace both springs since the other spring might be next to snap. The repairman arrived the next day, and I asked him if this was something that I could replace myself if this should ever happen again. He highly recommended that I should leave it to the professionals since the springs were under such a high amount of pressure. While watching him install the new springs, I fully agreed with him on that recommendation. He also recommended that we replace the torsion springs on both sides because if one goes the other one will soon follow. I decided to hold off, and within 30 days the other side broke.

Whenever I did any home inspections and the garage had torsion springs, I always shared this story to let them know what to expect and how to get it fixed.

On newer homes, reverse sensors are installed on the rails approximately 16 inches off the garage floor. These sensors are designed to notify the openers that someone or something has crossed the light beam and may be hurt if the door continues to close. The garage door will automatically reverse and cause the light on the motor to flash and acknowledge the sensors' response.

Also, the garage door should have an auto reverse feature in case something is blocking the door and not letting it completely close. The door will automatically reverse and the light on the motor will flash to acknowledge the blockage.

If the garage door of the home you're looking at does not have one, you should definitely have one installed. If the home does have the sensor, your home inspector will test it and make sure it is working properly.

11

HEALTH HAZARDS

1. Mold & Mildew

While working with a home improvement company, I had an
appointment up in Haverhill, Massachusetts. This client's home
was built in the mid-1700s and was in dire need of new windows.
In getting to know the client, he talked about his son waking up in
the middle of the night unable to breathe. This had been going on
over the past few weeks and his son was taken to the hospital and
released with no resolution to the problem. He further explained
that his wife was now experiencing the same symptoms and having
problems breathing.

I asked him if we could take a quick look into his attic. When
we entered the attic, I could not see any exposed wood because all
of it was covered with white mold. I told him that this was what
was causing the family's respiratory problems. There are three basic
types of molds: white, black, and green. All are due to extreme
moisture, and all can cause serious health issues. White mold is the
most dangerous because it causes severe respiratory issues. This
home condition is referred to as a "sick house." This is very dangerous and must be remedied immediately.

We will get into this more in the second half of this book, but while you're searching for a home, be on the lookout for spots on walls and ceilings and don't be shy about asking any questions.

2. *Radon Gas*

Quote from the EPA:

Radon comes from the breakdown of naturally occurring radioactive elements (such as uranium and thorium) in soils and rocks. As part of the radioactive decay process, radon gas is produced. The gas moves up through the soil to the surface, where it can enter homes, schools and the workplace through cracks and other holes in the foundation. In some cases, radon can enter buildings through well water and come from building materials. Any home can have a radon problem—old or new homes, well-sealed or drafty homes, and homes with or without basements.

Radon is a naturally occurring radioactive gas that can cause lung cancer. Radon gas is inert, colorless, and odorless. Radon is naturally in the atmosphere in trace amounts. Outdoors, radon disperses rapidly and, generally, is not a health issue. Most radon exposure occurs inside homes, schools, and workplaces. Radon gas becomes trapped indoors after it enters buildings through cracks and other holes in the foundation. Indoor radon can be controlled and managed with proven, cost-effective techniques.

Breathing radon over time increases your risk of lung cancer. Radon is the second leading cause of lung cancer in the United States. Nationally, the EPA estimates that about 21,000 people die each year from radon-related lung cancer. Only smoking causes more lung cancer deaths. You can take steps to reduce and control the amount of radon in your home. Testing is the only way to determine radon levels. Have your home tested, either by a professional or with a do-it-yourself home test kit. If radon levels are high, contact a certified radon service professional to fix your home. EPA guidance suggests mitigating if levels are at or above 148 Bq/m3 (4 pCi/L). Usually, radon problems are fixed using an underground ventilation system or by increasing the rate of air changes in the building.

STANDARD RADON MITIGATION SYSTEM

The way to remove radon gas from the home is by having a radon mitigation system installed. The base of the pipe is installed below the basement floor. Gas is then piped outside, and a low voltage motor is attached to push the radon gas up through the pipe, which is exposed to fresh air above the roofline. This motor is designed to run 24/7/365 and makes very little noise and does not cost much to run.

When you're looking for a new home for you and your family, look at other homes in the area and look for this radon gas mitigation system. If the house that you're looking at does not have this system and is surrounded by houses that do have it, more than likely the home you're looking at may need a mitigation system.

Depending on the state the home is located, homeowners may not be required to get a radon gas test done (please check your local state code requirements). Usually, the only time homeowners get the home tested is when they want to sell it and the buyers are asking for a radon test. Only then, when the test results come back and show a high level of radon, will the issue be resolved by either the sellers installing the system or a credit to the buyer at closing of the home to cover the cost (around $1,000-$1,500 depending on the size of the home and the area the home is located).

One of the homes I had built was a garrison/colonial; four-bedroom, two full baths, one half-bath, full basement with a two-car garage under. We lived there for approximately seven years and two of my neighbors came down with various types of cancer, along with myself.

I knew the person who bought the home and was invited back to visit a few years after I sold it. I noticed that the new homeowner had the home tested for radon (long after I sold it), and they had a radon mitigation system installed.

The EPA does recommend that a radon test be performed in the home every two years or when any major renovations are done. If the radon gas levels are found to be above acceptable levels and the remediation system needs to be installed, then the home should be tested annually.

Either way, if you're thinking of buying a new home or even staying with the home you're currently living in, get the home tested just for your own peace of mind. The test is very inexpensive and available at your local hardware store. I just bought one for my own house at the cost of $15.00.

12

ELECTRICAL

The picture shown above provides vital information on how your electricity and other utilities are delivered to your home. Just a quick note: the highest wires are carrying the high voltage and are the most dangerous. The high voltage lines then go through a step-down transformer, which reduces the voltage to 210-230 volts that flow through the secondary wires that feed to the local homes and businesses. Anytime voltage is reduced, it creates heat. These step-down transformers run very hot and are under a lot of pressure. I have seen firsthand what happens when these step-down transformers fail.

My wife and I were asleep one night, and a transformer located in a nearby plaza exploded and caught fire. It sounded like a cannon went off, and was so loud it woke us from a sound sleep.

When looking for a new home, a very important element to be aware of is your electrical service. Your home inspector should do a thorough inspection, but you should be aware of a few components.

Electricity comes to your home either by underground wiring or overhead wires. Having your electrical service coming into the home underground may look nice in your neighborhood but makes it very hard to determine where any kind of electrical break or shortage may happen. Having your electrical service coming to the home via overhead wiring creates its own set of concerns.

Again, the highest wires carry the electrical load from the electrical grid, and the second set of wires comes from the step-down transformer. The lower lines are communication wires, but either way overhead wiring is exposed to the weather 24/7/365. Extreme heat can make the lower wiring sag, causing it to be a possible hazard to larger trucks (good to know when you decide to move into a home and use a moving company or rent a truck and move yourselves).

Overhead electrical lines are also susceptible to being taken down by strong winds, ice storms, broken tree limbs, downed trees, and motor vehicle accidents. Knowing how the electrical service is coming to the home, and the accompanying potential problems, will help you decide on purchasing the home or just continuing with your search.

If your home is new, you may have an outdoor electrical main shutoff located right next to your electrical meter instead of in the interior electrical box. The reason that the main shutoff is now located on the exterior of the home is due to new 2020 electrical codes. This new code was motivated by EMS, local fire departments, and firefighters. When a fire is reported to the fire department and firefighters are dispatched, they would normally have to wait until the local electrical service is shut off to the home or take on the dangerous task of removing the electrical meter before flooding the home with water to put out the flames. Now the firefighters can locate the exterior electrical shutoff so they can put out the fire faster instead of waiting for the local electrical company to send out their trucks. The old way was to just remove the exterior meter to the home, which would kill the power to the home, but the open circuit would remain very dangerous to the firefighters while putting out the fire. Always treat any downed wires as if they were live. Do not touch or even go near them until emergency services either shut off the lines or remove them.

The problem is that anyone, including burglars and predators, can now shut off your electrical service and disarm any alarm system if there is no backup battery in the security systems. This would also shut off any video cameras that would show the burglars breaking into the home unless they have a battery backup.

This exterior switch has a waterproof cover but has a very small slot to put a small lock. Any small lock can easily be broken but it still is some type of deterrent.

If your power goes out, always check your neighborhood homes to make sure their power is also off, regardless of where your electrical shutoff is.

If you do have a newer system with an outdoor electrical main shutoff, and there is power in your neighborhood, I do not

recommend you going outside, especially at night, to investigate. Contact a neighbor or two and have them escort you to the electrical main. Now that burglars and predators are aware that your electrical shutoff is located outside, they can shut off your power knowing it will likely cause you or a loved one to go outside and investigate the problem. Again, this makes you vulnerable for an attack and/or home invasion.

Incoming electrical services per home will vary depending on the age of the home. A building that I purchased back in 1984 to start my childcare center was built over 100 years ago. When I purchased this home, I converted it to a childcare center and did many renovations over the course of the next 20 years. The electrical service when I purchased the home was only 60 amps with glass fuses, and I'm sure the family went through many fuses during their time living there. During one of the renovations, we had to upgrade the electrical service to 400 amp 3 phase just to carry the electrical load.

If you're looking at a home that the homeowners have lived in all their lives, you would be lucky if they did all the upgrades needed during the decades, such as a new roof, electrical, heating/AC, and plumbing. If you're inside the home, it is okay to ask your realtor to find out if, what, and when upgrades have been done over the many years of the current homeowners residing in the home.

I had one construction client that purchased their home back in the early '70s and was now interested in getting prices to upgrade all the electrical, windows, doors, siding, and roofing. He was shocked when I told him what the price would be to do all these upgrades, and his response was, "If I do this all my equity will be used to do all the upgrades." My response was that most homeowners know that the home needs constant attention, maintenance, and upkeep. If you don't do any of this over the course of time you're living in the home, the costs of these upgrades will be much more expensive, in part because more damage will be done due to delaying the necessary upgrades.

The electrical upgrade alone from his current 100-amp service to 200-amp service was approximately $3,000. Costs of all materials are constantly increasing, along with the labor to get these projects done. Anyone interested in purchasing the home will bring this up, along with any other deficiencies, and request a credit at the closing to upgrade the system.

It basically comes down to this: if a homeowner keeps their home in good condition by doing routine maintenance and upgrades, they can command a higher price for the home when they decide to sell it.

Again, surveys always have stated that families usually only stay in their homes for a period of 7 to 10 years. Always keep this in mind if you're considering doing any renovations to the home you're considering purchasing. So much can happen within that time, such as job relocation, family situations, health, growing children's needs, and an empty nest.

FYI: Electrical deaths are reported to be approximately 400 annually, with over 30,000 electrical injuries and over 25,000 electrical fires every year!

Wooden utility poles are usually made from Southern yellow pine, Douglas fir, or Western red cedar. The poles are usually 40 feet long, 6 feet in the ground and 34 feet aboveground. They are also coated with chemicals to prevent insect infestation and rotting.

Whenever wood meets any type of soil, tar, or cement; that is where the rotting process begins. Once this happens, the pole becomes weaker and less likely to get through high winds and storm damage.

If the house you're interested in has a pole near the house, just take a few minutes to look at the condition of the utility pole. Also keep in mind that either you or someone else on the street would need to report the decaying utility pole to your local utility company, and that it needs to be replaced. There are many YouTube videos on how the utility poles are made, so you may want to take a few minutes to educate yourselves.

A home that I inspected was set back from the road approximately 150 feet. Because of the distance, the span was too long to make an electrical run, so the utility company had to place a utility pole halfway up the property line. As with all other inspections, I inspected the pole and discovered that the guy wire that supported the stress on the pole was loose and dangling. I told the homeowners to call the local utility company and have them either reset the guy wire or tighten it up to take the stress off the pole.

13

PLUMBING

1. Incoming Water Supply

When researching a home, knowing where your incoming water is coming from and where your wastewater is discharged is essential.

Water and sewer services in most areas are provided by the local city or town. In other areas, cities or towns may just offer water supplied by the city or town and your home has its own septic or cesspool for wastewater. For homes in more rural areas, the home's incoming water may be drawn from a well located near the home, and the home also takes care of its own wastewater.

Incoming water lines from the local city or town are always under pressure. This is needed to move the water through the home to all the faucets, sinks, toilets, and showers. The picture shown above is the water meter and is attached to the incoming water line from the street to the home, with a shutoff valve at the street level and one in the actual home. This meter is also linked to an outside meter that the city or town can read to know how much to bill you for your water usage. Knowing the location of the shutoff valve is extremely important and shutting off both sides of the meter is recommended when needed.

The age of the home will determine what type of shutoff you'll have on either side of the above meter shown.

The picture on the left is called a ball valve and the picture on the right is called a gate valve. The gate valves are usually found on older homes and the ball valve is usually found on newer homes. Both work well, but usually because they are in dark dank places, over time the valves become stuck in the "on" position. It is advisable to turn these on and off at least once per year to keep them from sticking.

My next-door neighbor built his house over 30 years ago. He had to call the city water department to come and shut off the city water at the street shutoff. I noticed the city truck pull up while I was outside working on my own home, and I went over to talk to my neighbor. He informed me that he was trying to replace a toilet in the house. The toilet shutoff broke off, and when he tried to shut off the house water meter, that valve also broke off, causing flooding in the basement.

One of my clients owned a beautiful home in Rhode Island and another located in Florida. They were snowbirds who spent summers in Rhode Island and winters in Florida. They wanted a security system, including cameras and a water monitor. When I asked if there was a potential problem they were trying to avoid, she said that while they were in Florida, the finished basement was flooded due to a break in the waterline in the refrigerator located in the basement. I asked her if she shut off the water at the water meter while they were away, and her response was "What's that?" I then asked her if she had any kind of a utility room in the basement. She did and I located the water meter for her. I showed her how to shut the water meter off and informed her how much pressure the house is constantly under while the water main is left on. Interior hoses and plumbing can fail at any time and taking this precaution would have saved them a lot of grief, aggravation, and expense.

Another client built a million-dollar home on the water in Jamestown, Rhode Island. He decided to take his family to Disney World for three weeks and when he arrived back home, he discovered that half of his house was destroyed by water. He opened the front door and found the first-floor ceiling was now on the first-floor floor. He then went into the basement and found the basement ceiling was now on the basement floor. The entire left side of this beautiful home was completely destroyed by water. All the large picture window frames that overlooked the water had swelled, all the doorframes and doors also swelled, and even exterior damage was done to the home.

The leak was caused by a weak waterline connection and the water pressure eventually caused that weak connection to finally let go in the third-floor bathroom. The cost to repair this home was more than $300,000, and all this could have been avoided if the pressure was taken off the house while they were away.

I share these stories just to show you the importance of knowing where these valves are and the importance of their routine maintenance.

If the new home you're looking at is in a more rural area, the home may have its own water well. If the house water supply is served by a water well, I would highly suggest watching some YouTube videos to better understand how the water well was made and how the water well actually works.

Without getting into the engineering of the well, the cost of installing a water well is many thousands of dollars. Water wells may be as shallow as 50 feet and can go as deep as over 300 feet.

I have seen developers purchase homes with larger properties that they can subdivide and construct new homes on. They then make the choice to either sell the existing home or demolish it and construct a new house in its place. If they are selling the existing home and it has a water well, it may not be deep enough if other houses are being built and drawing from the same water supply. If the new homes also need one or more water wells, and if they draw large amounts of water, a term called "cone of depression" will take place. This "cone of depression" means that neighboring wells are pulling water from the aquifer and lowering the height of the water source, thus causing the existing home's water well to dry up. Just keep this in mind if you're in this position, because you may find yourselves having to pay for the installation of a new well.

This may be a negotiation tactic in your purchase and sale agreement; that money be put in escrow to cover the cost of a new well in case the new development is drawing too much water. After the development is completed and a certain amount of agreed upon time has passed, then the fund could be released back to the seller.

The home inspectors usually don't do inspections on water well systems, so I would highly advise you to have the well and water inspected by a professional service company.

2. Wastewater

Wastewater from a home is removed in a variety of ways: private septic system and leach field, macerated and pumped and/or gravity fed into a public sewer system, macerated and/or pumped into a gravity fed private system on the same site as the home.

If the house is serviced by the city's sewer services, the sewer line from the home is fed into this system, usually located on the street which other houses are tied into. The wastewater is then pumped to a local treatment plant for processing. In my opinion, this is the best way for the homeowner to get rid of all the wastewater. It may cost a few hundred dollars every year for this service, but it is well worth avoiding the headaches of a private system.

Whether the home has a public or a private system, each has clean-out traps inside and outside of the home. These clean-out traps are an essential part of the wastewater system in case any blockage occurs.

If the home you're looking at has a basement that you're thinking about renovating into living space, always make sure that you do not block those clean-out traps in case of a blockage. Either make an access door or purchase one at your local hardware store.

PVC PIPING & CAST IRON PIPING

In newer homes, PVC piping is used both inside and outside. This piping is very thick and durable, but if heavy equipment is driven over the pipe, it will break and leak into the soil. If the pipe is crushed, the home's plumbing will back up and cause the homeowners a major headache, cost, and aggravation.

In older homes, cast-iron piping was used to remove wastewater. This cast-iron piping is very strong and durable, but over time the piping will eventually rot out and do so from the inside out. You'll never know until it fails and starts to leak. Once again, keeping an eye on your plumbing lines and fixtures occasionally will save you a lot of grief and aggravation.

3. Cesspools

With private cesspool and septic systems, the system is now 100 percent the responsibility of the homeowners. A cesspool is basically just a deep hole in the ground with a pipe coming out of the house. This is the how the cesspool system works:

1. Waste flows from the home into the cesspool.
2. Organic solids float to the top and inorganic solids sink to the bottom of the tank.
3. Naturally occurring bacteria in the cesspool converts the organic solids to liquid.
4. The clear liquid flows out the sides of the tank and into the surrounding soil.
5. Annual pumping out of the solids that sink to the bottom of the cesspool is highly recommended to avoid buildup and cesspool failure.

I just renovated a home in the summer and fall of 2020 that had not been lived in for over three years which has an existing cesspool. After having the city water turned back on and getting the faucets and bathroom running again, there was a gurgling sound coming from the floor under the toilet. The house is built on a slab, so I knew we had our work cut out for us. I decided to call in a company to pump out the cesspool. After uncovering the cesspool, we discovered that it was bone dry, so the next move was to contact a drain cleaning company to clear out the drain coming from the house.

The drain cleaning company found a tree root inside the pipe that, after being removed, measured about six feet long and two inches thick. Other debris was removed and the flow from the home to the cesspool was finally cleared and operational.

It is not uncommon to find tree roots growing through sewer and septic system piping. If you find yourselves in this situation where your plumbing is not flowing or backing up, get a plumber to help clean the blockage. If the blockage is outside of the home, some plumbers can clear the pipe; if not, then other professional companies will snake and clear the pipes with much larger and more sophisticated equipment.

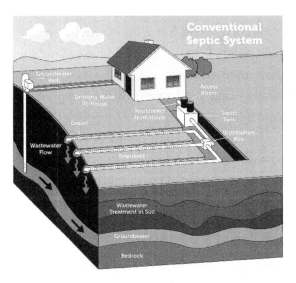

4. Septic Systems

Copied from the EPA:

Specifically, this is how a typical conventional septic system works:

1. *All water runs out of your house from one main drainage pipe into a septic tank.*
2. *The septic tank is a buried, water-tight container usually made of concrete, fiberglass, or polyethylene. Its job is to hold the wastewater long enough to allow solids to settle down to the bottom, forming sludge, while the oil and grease floats to the top as scum.*
3. *Compartments and a T-shaped outlet prevent the sludge and scum from leaving the tank and traveling into the drain field area.*
4. *The liquid wastewater (effluent) then exits the tank into the drain field.*
5. *The drain field is a shallow, covered, excavation made in unsaturated soil. Pre-treated wastewater is discharged through piping onto porous surfaces that allow wastewater to filter through the soil. The soil accepts, treats, and disperses wastewater as it percolates through the soil, ultimately discharging to groundwater. If the drain field is overloaded with too much liquid, it can flood, causing sewage to flow to the ground surface or create backups in toilets and sinks.*
6. *Finally, the wastewater percolates into the soil, naturally removing harmful coliform bacteria, viruses, and nutrients. Coliform bacteria are a group of bacteria predominantly inhabiting the intestines of humans or other warm-blooded animals. It is an indicator of human fecal contamination.*

FAILURE SYMPTOMS: MIND THE SIGNS!

A foul odor is not always the first sign of a malfunctioning septic system. Call a septic professional if you notice any of the following:

- *Wastewater backing up into household drains.*
- *Bright green, spongy grass on the drain field, especially during dry weather.*
- *Pooling water or muddy soil around your septic system or in your basement.*
- *A strong odor around the septic tank and drain field.*

Outside of public sewer systems, septic systems are the most used system for disposing of wastewater. The downside of this system is that it requires a large area for the septic tank and the leaching field. If you're looking at a home and are thinking about putting up a pool or any type of building in the future, it cannot be placed over the tank or leaching field. This also includes expanding your driveway or parking areas, which cannot be placed over the leach field. There are commercial applications currently used that allow parking lots to be placed over leaching fields, but they are very expensive and not economical for residential use.

When a home is renovated to add more living space (especially bedrooms and bathrooms), usually the city or town requires that the septic system be inspected, or a copy of the system design be submitted. They're looking to see if the septic system is designed and big enough to handle the added bathrooms and water usage from the homeowners. They assume that since the homeowners are doing renovations that more people will be moving in and taxing the existing system. Depending on their findings, the city or town may require the homeowners to replace the septic system to accommodate the added water usage.

I've seen and heard too many horror stories of people purchasing their home with the idea of adding additional square footage to handle their families. When they go through the exhaustive paperwork, engineering costs and plans, they find out that they need to spend another estimated $15,000 to $30,000. Sometimes they don't even have enough space to increase the system and must look into newer environmental systems that use less space, but that may cost even more.

Just keep in mind when you're purchasing a home that you may want your real estate agent or broker to ask specific questions about the septic system. Some of which are who and how many people are currently living in the home, how old is the septic system, and how often have the current owners had their system pumped and maintained? In most states, a septic system inspection is required and noted in the purchase and sale agreement, but doing your own due diligence is highly recommended.

If the septic system test is done and the septic system fails, a report will be given to the proper parties. There are times that this may put the sale of the house on hold or even stop the sale completely because the current homeowners can't afford to have it fixed or replaced. The option of the current owners putting money aside in an escrow account at the closing can be done to satisfy both the buyer and the seller. This option would allow the sale to go through and not have to wait for a contractor to replace the septic system.

If you're looking for a home on or near the water, other agencies will get involved. Federal agencies like the EPA (Environment Protection Agency) and the US Army Corps of Engineers get involved with anything on or near our waterways. Getting permission to build any structure on or near the water may take years, a boatload of money, and an unbelievable amount of paperwork and engineering drawings.

There are many other types of "ecosystems" that are designed for smaller plots of land but need more maintenance. Some of these systems even have electrical requirements for them to run. If you're looking at a home with one of these systems, do your homework and find out what the required maintenance might be.

It's very important to know that the only time a garbage disposal can be installed is in a home that has town water and sewer. If the home has a garbage disposal installed under the kitchen sink without town water and sewerage, then all that waste is now going into the septic system or cesspool, and they are not designed to handle food. How long that garbage disposal has been installed will determine just how much damage has been done to the septic system or cesspool. You may not notice any problems for a while, but eventually you may be blocking your leach field or cesspool.

I have replaced a few garbage disposals in my own homes. Even though the instructions say that it's okay to put bones in the disposal, this really taxes the disposal and shakes all the piping under the sink, possibly doing damage to the disposal and plumbing. I would rather put the bones in the trash and send softer foods down the disposal while washing the dinner dishes.

5. Hot Water Tanks

Every home has the need and demand for hot water for showers, baths, sinks and laundry machines. Water heating systems come in a wide variety of sizes and shapes. Some are heated inside tanks that can be heated by natural gas, electricity, and even oil. Newer systems now have tankless on-demand water heaters that heat the water as it's being used.

Older homes are usually serviced by hot water tanks that run on natural gas, electricity, or oil. Electric tanks don't need any type of venting, but oil and natural gas water heaters need to be properly vented because of the carbon monoxide being created by the tank.

When looking at an older home, look at the tank and see what condition it is in. On average, an electric hot water tank will last anywhere from 10 to 15 years. An oil or natural gas water tank should last anywhere from 8 to 12 years. Keep this in mind when making your decision to purchase the home.

Poorly handled maintenance can add new dangers. One time a new homeowner contacted me to upgrade their alarm system. They'd just moved into this new $400,000 home. I went down to the basement to see their existing system and, when I arrived in the basement, I got a big whiff of natural gas. I went over to the gas water heater and the smell got more intense. I immediately got the new homeowners to come down to the basement and they told me that the sellers just had the tank replaced the day before. I told her that she needed to contact the installer immediately. She did and they arrived within 15 minutes. The installer did not tighten the gas line tight enough, nor did they test it for any leaks.

Electric hot water tanks are usually cheaper to purchase and install. The downside is that it is much more expensive to operate than an oil or natural gas tank. Because the tank does not require any venting, it can be placed in more confined areas such as closets, cabinets (depending on the size), garages, or basements.

Oil fired hot water tanks use the same type of oil that's used in the home heating system. If you see one fuel line coming from the oil tank, it's usually attached to a splitter that branches off to both the burner and the hot water tank.

At times, the hot water tank may be strapped to the wall. These straps are called "earthquake straps," for obvious reasons, in certain areas of the country which encounter earthquakes. I have seen these straps placed on tanks in areas not prone to earthquakes, so don't be alarmed if you see one on the tank in the home you're looking at. Some plumbers like to make sure the tank won't fall over because it really is very top-heavy.

The above picture shown is what may happen when a hot water tank is not installed correctly. This picture is of a test of what could happen when a hot water tank becomes over pressured; it exploded and went through the ceiling joists and roof and kept going.

Never, never, *never* have anyone but a licensed plumber replace or install the temperature pressure release valve. Safety protocols are in place to balance the temperature of the tank and the water pressure of the tanks.

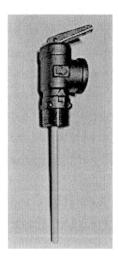

The picture shown is a picture of a temperature pressure relief valve. You'll find these on all types of hot water tanks. This valve can either be attached on the top or on the side of hot water tanks. This valve is designed to drain only when the hot water in the tank is over pressurized, or the temperature is too high. If this valve starts to leak, immediately locate a plumber to have them find out why it's leaking and replace the valve. A few reasons it could leak are outside temperature and pressure, the expansion tank may have gone bad or isn't even installed, anode rods may need to be replaced in the tank, or even the tank itself needs to be replaced. Any plumbing needed to be done to the hot water tank should be left to the professionals.

FYI: If the city or town your looking to purchase provides water to this home, be aware that there are times during the year that the fire hydrants need to be flushed out. When this flushing is done, brown water may appear in the home during or after the flushing is done. In order to clear out the lines in the home, only use the cold water faucet and toilets to flush out your incoming water lines. If you use the hot water, all this brown sediment will be pumped into the tank and need to be flushed out as well using a large amount of water.

If you're looking at a home and happen to see the hot water tank, just look at this valve and see if it shows any signs of leaking. Whatever you do, do not touch this valve! If you decide to move forward with the purchase of the home, your home inspector will take pictures of this and explain this valve in further detail if you just ask them.

14

HEATING SYSTEMS

When looking to purchase a home, knowing what type of heating and cooling systems the house has is of vital importance. The following information is a short overview of nontechnical information on the types of systems currently available and most commonly used. There are so many new and more economical systems coming into the market, but again these systems shown above are just a few of the basics you may see.

A friend of mine's family owns a plumbing and heating business. When a client calls in for a service call for their heating system, they are asked a specific question: "Do you have a boiler or a burner?" Then the client asks "What's the difference?" This is a strange answer when the client already owns the house, to not even know what type of system heats it.

There is always a new type of heating system that comes out on the market every year. Research is ongoing to make existing systems more economical to run in order to lower our carbon emissions. But the basic systems are run by natural or bottled gas, oil, or electricity.

Both systems look similar to the untrained eye. The difference between a boiler and a burner is in the name: a boiler boils water that is circulated through the house and a burner burns fuel that circulates the water throughout the home. Both systems can run on oil, or natural or bottled gas. In some instances, the water may be mixed with some type of antifreeze to keep the water from freezing in case power is lost and temperature goes below freezing.

In the school that I used to own, we had one area near the attic that would freeze when the outside temperature went below the freezing point. To keep this from happening, the service technician added antifreeze and the problem magically went away.

Home inspectors are not technicians, and only have basic knowledge regarding boilers and burners. It is also recommended during our training that you should not test a heating system in the middle of the summer, or test the air conditioning system during the wintertime. Taking this risk may cause damage to the system and possibly cause the current homeowners to go after the home inspector for damages. This being the case, it is a good idea to have a licensed technician check out the burner or boiler during the due diligence period.

1. Heating—Venting—Air Conditioning Systems (AKA—HVAC Systems)

HVAC systems offer the convenience of having one unit that both heats and cools the home during the various seasons. The heating system can run on oil, natural or bottled gas, or electricity. The cooling system "condenser" is a major part of the system. The

condenser draws out the hot air from the home and returns cool air through the air handler back into house.

Again, this information I'm sharing is just the basics of the system. There are many other moving parts, but just an overview is being done in this book. These systems come in various shapes and sizes, but the system is rated for the size of the home the system is installed in. I've been told by HVAC technicians that if a higher rated system is installed in the home that it has to work harder than one that is properly rated. The reason is that if a larger system is installed, it would cool down the home faster but would constantly

be cycling and using more electricity, causing excess wear and tear on the system. The HVAC system that is rated properly runs longer but doesn't have to cycle as often and keeps the wear and tear on the system down.

A dirty air conditioning compressor makes the unit work harder and does not cool down the house properly. This happened to our own home. When I had an a/c technician check it out, he took off the exterior grill and this is what we discovered. They use a special chemical that dissolves the dirt, and it just rinses off. The coolant was then recharged, and the system has been fine ever since.

Knowing this information will help you understand what to watch for if the home has an HVAC system. Again, you should feel free to ask questions about the system. When was it installed? Does it service the entire home? How often has it been serviced?

2. Chimneys and Fireplaces

It is very important to keep the flue closed when the fireplace is not being used. In May of 2021, a flock of migrating birds flew down a chimney in California and, because the flue was open, the birds were able to get into the home.

A chimney top or cover is designed to keep birds and small animals out of the chimney. It's also designed to keep rainwater, snow, leaves, and ice from going down inside the chimney. If any flammable debris makes its way inside the chimney, it may cause a chimney fire, which is very dangerous for your home.

The "chimney effect" is the movement of air in and out of a building or home. The chimney is always higher than the tallest part of the roof for a few reasons. The basic chimney effect is that higher winds cross over the chimney and draw air from inside the home (the fireplace) to the outside air. The height also keeps any possible cinders that may fly out of the chimney high enough to be taken away from the home instead of landing on the roof and causing a fire there.

Many newer homes have metal flues for any type of heating units inside the home, so basically no maintenance is needed. With brick-and-mortar chimneys, they may need to be re-pointed, which is basically repairing or replacing the mortar that has dried and/or fallen out. Also, proper flashing, a metal sheet installed where the chimney meets the roof to ensure a watertight connection, may be needed as well.

If you decide to purchase a home with a chimney, make sure you look for these problems and talk to your home inspector on what needs to be done.

15

INSECT AND PEST CONTROL

When you're looking at a home you may want to purchase, you usually never know if there is any type of insect living in the home. One of the things home inspectors look for is mud tubes climbing up from the ground or foundation, which attach themselves to the foundation and find their way under the siding and into the home. Other things we can see includes wood-boring insect damage, like from post beetles that eat at home structures.

If you have any other suspicion that there may be an intrusion of any insects or rodents, contact a professional to check out the home during the due diligence time allowed.

In one of the homes I owned, paper wasps decided to infest my home over the front door. They dug a hole in the clapboard siding and made a good-sized nest. I had to contact a professional exterminator to take care of this because it is recommended not to spray anything in the nest; these wasps are known to attack anything or anyone who comes near.

If you come across a home that has anthills (maybe not as severe as the lawn in this picture), it's very possible that the home may be infested as well. Ants need food to sustain themselves—where are they getting it from?

If you're still interested in investing in this home, make sure you hire an experienced pest control company to check out the home and find out the cost to get rid of all the anthills and maintain a routine schedule for pest control.

Even though these mice look cute, they can do a lot of damage. I built a 10-by-10-foot shed in the back of our yard a few years ago that stores all our outdoor furniture and pool supplies. We put all the furnishings and supplies inside in the fall and didn't open the shed until April the following year. Unbeknownst to us, the field mice had a field day in the shed and did over $500 worth of damage. They ate through our umbrellas, furniture, pool toys, card-board, and even through plastic bins. They even built a nest inside our outdoor heater that I was unable to take out, so we just ended up tossing it in the trash.

Your home inspector can usually find mice droppings and report them to you during your home inspection. But, if you see mousetraps while you're walking through the home, make sure you ask why they have them.

I have found quite a few mousetraps during home inspections, but they usually were found inside bulkhead doors. Mice can squeeze into very small holes and get into the home; having mouse-traps in that area usually stops them from getting any further.

While mice droppings may indicate a rodent problem, they can also make you very sick. The same goes for mouse urine, both of which are commonly used to mark territory. Mice spread diseases such as hantavirus, salmonella, and lymphocytic choriomeningitis (LCMC) through their waste, even if you are careful not to touch them.

Hantavirus: Mouse feces and urine can dry and turn to dust, spreading viruses through the air we breathe. Hantavirus is commonly spread this way and can cause fever, chills, aches, and pains. If left untreated, it can progress to kidney failure and intense short-ness of breath.

Salmonella: Mice may track waste debris, along with dirt and bac-teria, across countertops. This is a common cause of salmonella (aka food poisoning), as we may touch kitchen surfaces while preparing food. Symptoms like fever, stomach pain, vomiting, and diarrhea can become serious.

Lymphocytic Choriomeningitis (LCMV): This is a viral infection that is typically carried by house mice and can cause serious neu-rological problems. Humans become infected through exposure to fresh mouse droppings, urine, saliva, and nesting materials.

16

POOLS

Aboveground and in-ground pools come in very wide varieties and sizes. Both are considered an asset and liability, depending on who is interested in purchasing the home.

Aboveground pools and newer in-ground pools usually have thick vinyl liners. Older in-ground pools usually have cement or ceramic lining to hold and handle the weight of the pool water.

Some of the advantages of an in-ground pool are that they are much more pleasing to the eye as far as landscaping. In talking to a good friend of mine, he said that he loves his in-ground pool, but he always finds rodents and snakes that get stuck in his pool skimmer.

Maintaining a pool can be an expensive and labor-intensive chore, so please take time to think about how you can balance your time to maintain the pool chemical levels and constant cleaning. Also, know that maintaining this pool is a year-round responsibility, because even when the pool is closed, keeping the pool cover clean and dry keeps the pool safe.

Proper fencing to protect you, your family, friends, and neighbors is mandatory in all parts of the country. Check with your local building department to ensure local laws are followed and that the heights of the fence are correct. Pools are considered an "attractive nuisance," which means that children are drawn to the water and may try to find ways to enter the pool. This pool is your responsibility, and if something happens to any neighbor, family, or friend, it is your responsibility.

A former neighbor of mine purchased a house near us that needed many renovations. After renovating the house, she decided to put in an in-ground pool and landscape the entire backyard. She rented it for a few years then decided to sell it. The new owner, who had a young family, decided to bring in an excavator and fill in the in-ground pool and changed the landscaping in the backyard.

Which part of the country you live in will help determine if you want to have it heated to get a longer season out of it. As we get older, it becomes less tolerable to deal with the cold-water temperatures, so heating was our decision when installing our pool back in 2010.

A few things that our pool salesperson neglected to tell us when we purchased the pool: You need to place a mat under the pool ladder to prevent the movement of the ladder from wearing out and causing holes in the liner. Also, the mat helps to keep small rocks in the sand bottom from working their way through the liner. Unfortunately, we weren't aware that this was happening to the pool liner, but we were constantly having to add water to the pool. We finally realized what had happened and had to replace the liner before the next pool season.

After doing much research, we discovered that there is a blanket that can be installed below the liner bottom to protect it from rocks tearing through. Also, since we heat our pool, we purchased insulation that is placed between the liner and the sides of the pool. By doing these two inexpensive things, we cut our pool heating costs in half and have extended the life of our pool liner.

In the interest of saving time learning how pool filters work, do your homework and see what type of filtration system the current owners are using and the approximate cost of maintaining the pool and chemical levels. If you're interested in purchasing the home and want to install a pool there, research the local zoning laws on where the pool can be located and if there are any size restrictions based on the size of the property.

17

FENCING

As a Certified Home Inspector, it is not a requirement that we inspect fencing located around the home. With that being said, I have worked with homeowners and discussed the condition of the fence that is surrounding the home they're interested in purchasing.

The most common place a fence will fail is where the support posts meet the ground. Wood being exposed to soil and moisture will rot underground over time and eventually become so weak that a windstorm will knock it down. When I walk around the property with the owner, this is the first place I look to discover possible rot and future failure.

Even if you're young with a strong back and want to install a fence yourself (speaking from experience because I *have* done this myself), it is very difficult to dig the holes and align the posts and panels in a perfect straight line. Hire the pros who do this every day and save your backs!

Although there are many different types of fencing (brick, block, stone), the three most popular types of fencing are wood, vinyl, and metal. They all come in a very wide variety of sizes, shapes, and durability.

Wood fencing is the most popular and least expensive to purchase, but the panels come in different types of wood. The cheapest is pine and it discolors quickly, shrinks and warps within a very short period of time. With the less expensive fencing, the posts installed to support the fence panels should be pressure treated. Other woods used like cedar, redwood, cypress, and oak fence panels are more expensive but last much longer, and are less likely to shrink and warp over time. If you let any type of panel age on its own it will reduce the life of the fencing. Do your research on what types of preservatives are available and which type and color you may want to use.

Vinyl fencing was very expensive when it originally came on the market back in the 1990s, but as with everything else, manufacturers have found less expensive ways to manufacture vinyl siding. Unfortunately, they use a cheaper grade to keep the cost down.

Metal fencing has been around for hundreds of years, but again, manufacturers have discovered cheaper ways to manufacture the metal fencing to make it more affordable to homeowners. As with other types of fencing, metal/aluminum fencing comes in a wide variety of shapes, sizes, and durability levels. Metal fencing is usually far more expensive than vinyl, but that depends on the quality of the fence panels and support posts.

From a security standpoint, nontransparent fencing is both an asset and a liability. A nontransparent fence allows you and your home privacy, but it also gives potential burglars a place to hide.

Metal and chain-link fences are fully transparent and inexpensive ways to protect your home, but do not allow any privacy.

OWNING A HOME
INTRODUCTION

Views vary on why you should purchase a home instead of renting. It was a common practice and understanding that the best opportunity was not to rent because you're paying someone else's mortgage payment. You're giving the landlord the capability of paying down or paying off their mortgage payment on the property, so obviously purchasing your own home allows you to pay down and pay off your own mortgage.

Back in the late 1990s I had to pick up my now ex-wife and one of my sons, who had gone on a Disney cruise, at the Providence Airport in Rhode Island. After arriving and parking my car, I discovered that the flight coming back to Providence was delayed for two hours. After a few choice words in my mind, I decided to go to the gift shop and see if I could find something to read while I was waiting. I noticed a book titled *Rich Dad—Poor Dad* that caught my attention. I read the back cover and it looked very appealing, so I bought it. I found a seat in the airport waiting area and could not put it down. I finished over 50 pages before the flight arrived. After I got the family home, I went to bed reading the book and finished it the next day.

The book was written by Robert Kiosaki and I highly recommend you purchase this book and share it with as many people as you can. The premise is based on your perceptions of how money is made, how it is spent, the difference between an asset and a liability, and what this man learned through his lifetime about the actual concept of money.

One of the major things I learned was that your home is not an asset, it is a liability. Assets make you money and liabilities cost you money. What would happen if you do not pay your mortgage payment? The bank will repossess it and leave you without your home.

If you don't pay your city or town real estate taxes, the city or town will take your home and sell it at a tax sale to recuperate the taxes owed. Trust me when I tell you that there are many people and companies making a ton of money on buying foreclosed and tax sale homes, and it happens all over the country. When you start to understand this concept of money, you realize that, no matter if you pay *a* mortgage or pay off *your* mortgage, you still will never really own your home. It all goes back to the days of the kings owning all the land in the kingdom. Everyone had to pay taxes to the king to keep their homes on his land.

Robert Kiosaki has published many books and I've read most of them. I still apply these concepts today and have guided many other investors buying assets such as income property, which will pay for your liabilities such as your homes, vehicles, and other toys and hobbies you may have. Again, I highly recommend taking some time to read these books and start with his first published book.

Another point I'm trying to make is it is not usually the price of your home, it is the repayment structure. If you're able to afford the home and not going without furniture for a few years then move ahead and enjoy the journey. I'm sure your bank or financing company will guide you on what you can afford so I won't address this in the book. Hopefully your home will increase in value over time, which will increase your equity. Just understand that, as your equity increases, so does that of every other homeowner's property. So, if you're looking to relocate, just remind yourself that you're also going to pay more for the next home.

18

MOVING IN

Now that you've decided to purchase your new home, knowing how it works and ways to keep you and your family safe are major concerns. The age of the home will determine how much you'll need to do to accomplish this.

One of the very first things you should do is replace all the locks and deadbolts in the house. Don't rely on the keys from the former owner. You don't know how many other people have a copy of those keys. Also, if you have a garage with a garage door opener, make sure you change all the codes in the main unit and on the remotes.

After all the furniture is moved in and in place, the members of the household can start to get acclimated to your new home. As with other places you've lived, getting used to new noises in the home will take some time. In older homes, the water lines and heating lines aren't always supported properly and will make noises when running. With an HVAC system, sometimes just the running of the fan motor may take some getting used too. How far set back your house is will determine just how much road noise you'll be hearing.

19

SAFETY

As I stated in the first introduction in this book, with my many experiences, I have so much information to share regarding safety.

So, you replaced all the locks and deadbolts, reprogrammed the garage openers and remotes, but you still have many more projects ahead of you.

One of my clients asked to have an alarm system with cameras installed in their home. When I arrived, the homeowners shared the reason they were interested in an alarm system. One night, their son had come home around midnight and opened the right-side door of a two-car garage to get in. He discovered that his brand-new $10,000 motorcycle was missing from the garage. They had the police investigate the stolen motorcycle, but interestingly, there was no evidence of a break-in anywhere in the garage or home.

Wanting to uncover this mystery, I googled how to break into a garage overhead door. I was amazed that YouTube had a video on how to break into an overhead garage door in less than 30 seconds. I highly suggest you watch this video just so you'll realize that burglars are always working on new ways to invade your home.

Hopefully during your move in, some of your neighbors have

been over to introduce themselves (at least that was the way it was when I was much younger). These days, you'll be lucky to even meet your neighbors at all. My advice is to go and meet your neighbors and get their contact information. I'll share this story of what happened to one of my clients:

A client in Lincoln, Rhode Island called in wanting a security system installed in his home. When I arrived, he informed me that he bought the model home from the development company and had been there for five years. I asked him the reason for contacting me, and he informed me that he was just broken into last night. The burglars broke through a window in the basement, went up to the second floor, and stole approximately $5,000 worth of his wife's jewelry. He then informed me that he spoke to his neighbor the next day and informed him of what happened. His neighbor then asked him if this happened about 4:00 p.m., because he noticed a painting van parked outside of his home!

I share this story because burglars are now disguising themselves as contractors. They drive up in trucks or vans with roof racks that carry the extension ladders they need to get up to the second floor of the house. I'll get into this further during the "Security System" section as to why homeowners should arm the second floor as well as the first floor and basements.

Meeting his neighbors in the immediate area and opening communication would have saved this homeowner a lot of grief and money. You should also suggest open communication with your neighbors. If you see something that might be suspicious like a moving van or contractor showing up (and you know your neighbor is not home), it's okay to contact them to make sure everything is okay.

Also, in introducing yourselves to your neighbors, you should find out if they have any children. Parents love to talk about their children and usually volunteer their ages. Being a good neighbor is also watching over your neighbors' children while you're outside of your own home. Child abductions can happen very quickly, so help keep an eye out for all your neighbors.

Over time you'll start to determine your neighbors' routines and schedules. What time they leave and come home from work, what time their children go to and from school, what time the children go out and play and where, who, and what cars usually come to visit them. You'll learn to look for a strange vehicle on the street with a person just sitting there. I like to call this being a "nice nosy neighbor."

Many times while I had an appointment, I would show up at least 15 minutes before the appointment and just wait outside in my truck. I did this for a few reasons, one being I wanted to study the neighborhood, and the other was to determine just how concerned their neighbors were with a strange person parked outside with the engine running.

A few times I was approached by neighbors walking by and sometimes I had homeowners come out of their homes to see who I was and why I was parked there. I did show my credentials and thanked them for approaching me for the safety of their neighborhood. I would then tell the homeowners of my appointment what their neighbors did, and that they should do the same. Even if they did not want to approach a vehicle, they should call the local police department and tell them about the strange vehicle with an unknown person inside. Believe it or not, I've had a few cruisers stop by and check me out!

One instance when I was waiting outside for an appointment, I noticed two children riding their bikes a few houses away. I was checking my phone when I heard a knock on my window, and these two children (approximately 8 and 10) asked me if I was lost and needed some help. Although I appreciate these young children asking me if I needed assistance, it also scared me knowing that if I was a child abductor, I could have caught at least one of them and the parents would never see them again. Again, I share these stories to make you aware of what does happen in today's world. There are approximately 460,000 children reported missing every year, so please teach your children not to approach strange vehicles.

Teaching children, even teenagers, how to be safe outside of the home can save their lives. All of us have taken risks and were lucky enough to get through it; I know of others who weren't so lucky. Back when I was a teenager (a very long time ago), my neighbor's teenage daughter snuck out of the house one night and went for a joyride with her friend. They were involved in a vehicle accident and both driver and passenger died in the crash. Another unlicensed teenager went for a joyride and lost control of the vehicle and crashed into my neighbor's cement foundation and ended up with permanent head trauma.

1. House Numbering

Having your house number very visible from the street in both the daytime and nighttime is of vital importance. Some may ask why but, coming from a law enforcement background and working directly with EMS, being able to locate a home in case of an emergency could be a matter of life or death.

Usually, house numbering has even numbers on one side of the street and odd numbers on the other, but sometimes homes are not numbered in numerical order. Construction or destruction of a house can disrupt that order in both rural and residential neighborhoods. This happened in our neighborhood; a house was constructed between my house and my neighbor's. So, we just determined that the city decided to use a number that should have been at the end of the street and put it next to ours. Now I'm sure that the city did not notify EMS that this strange house number is in the middle of the street. Thank goodness our neighbor was smart enough to put his house number on the mailbox and on the house.

Having your house numbered is also important for the post office and for package delivery companies. In working around my home, I've been asked a few times by delivery companies if I knew where a certain house or family was located. GPS is always helpful, but I've still had problems locating homes for some of my appointments.

2. Security Systems—Monitored vs Non-Monitored Systems

A non-monitored security system is considered a security system that only alarms the occupants while in their own home. If a break-in occurs when no one is home, no one outside of the home will be aware of what is happening unless you have outdoor sirens. The same situation occurs if there is a carbon monoxide leak or fire.

A monitored alarm system is a system that constantly watches over your home while you're at home or away. Whether the system is a basic system or complex system, both are monitored the same way. When the alarm is activated, the system makes a call to a monitoring station that calls the homeowners to see if there is an actual emergency or not. If the homeowners do not answer the proper phone number, the monitoring station contacts the local authorities, be it fire or police. Also, if the monitoring station contacts the homeowners and they use the wrong ID or code, they will automatically contact the proper authorities. I have seen firsthand during my training in Dallas, Texas what the call monitor operators are trained to say and do during these calls, and it is very impressive.

In today's world a security system is a must. I have met with so many families that have been burglarized, assaulted, and threatened from all walks of life.

When I met with all these families, I share my own story as to why you need a security system. In my younger days, I had moved a few times and built a few homes and had alarm systems installed.

The last house I built was in Hopedale, Massachusetts and was located at the top of a very large hill. Well, I was tired of paying the monthly monitoring fees, so I decided not to install a security system (it will never happen to me).

Exactly one year later, I came home late November around 6:00 p.m., walked up the stairs from the basement garage and found that the house was very cold. I walked into the kitchen and the sliding glass door was shattered in pieces all over the kitchen floor. There was a crack in the kitchen tile floor. I then looked to my left and, in the formal living room, the sectional couch had a long rip in the fabric, and on the floor was a rock about the size of small football with sharp jagged edges.

These intruders then went upstairs and stole approximately $25,000 worth of jewelry that was passed down on my ex-wife's side. I also had a tall plastic Coke bottle about 30 inches high filled with coins stolen. Then to top this off, they took my police hat off the top shelf from the closet and placed it in the middle of the floor, as if to say 'F#$%#$$% YOU! Police were called and investigated the home invasion, but they were never caught.

I ask my clients to please learn from my mistakes and understand that it's not a matter of "if," it's a matter of "when."

Having worked with the largest security company in the country and being trained to design sophistic security and video surveillance systems, my position was with the Custom Homes Division. This division works with high-profile clients and houses worth anywhere from $400 thousand to $2 million. I also designed smaller systems for smaller homes that needed protection.

One of these clients was a prison guard at the local ACI in Rhode Island. This officer was approached by a gang member who informed him that he was being released the following week, that he knew where the officer lived and that he was coming after him and his family. This officer had a wife and four children of various ages and lived on a highly traveled road. His concern was that he worked various shifts and wanted to keep an eye on his family while he was working. We designed a system that he was comfortable with and would keep his family safe.

Another client's son was murdered, thought to be part of gang retaliation. They were concerned that their family was next and wanted a secure system in place in their home.

I had a boyfriend/girlfriend situation whereby they bought an existing home deep in the woods in western Rhode Island. After they moved in, a fight ensued and the boyfriend moved out, but threatened to return with violent intentions. She asked me to design a system that she could monitor remotely with indoor and outdoor cameras.

My challenge was that she lived so deep in the woods, and that her driveway was partially hidden and narrow. Knowing that anything could happen with all three shifts of the police station, and that many different officers might be called to the scene, they would need assistance to locate the home. This also applies to firefighters and rescue crews if called. Knowing that in the summertime officers and firefighters may keep their windows open to listen for any noises, and knowing that in the wintertime all those officers and firefighters keep those windows closed, I designed a system that had both exterior sirens and flashing beacons.

One of my friends is an attorney in Connecticut with a 5,000-square-foot home. He asked me to design a system to protect it. Within one year, a dehumidifier overheated in his basement while he was at his daughter's soccer game. His mother-in-law stayed home and was asleep on the couch in their living room. The smoke alarms alerted the local fire department, which was able to get the mother-in-law out of the home and put out the fire. Although I received a Lifesaving Award for designing the system, I am so happy his family and home were safe.

I was called by my manager while on the road a few summers ago, and he informed me to stop whatever I was doing and head over to a home in Providence, Rhode Island. A phone call came in from an FBI agent in Washington, DC that his mother's home was just invaded and that she needed a security system installed immediately. A burglar broke into the back kitchen window, crawled over the kitchen sink, went upstairs, and stole some jewelry from another bedroom. He ended up in her bedroom and stood over her until the dog finally woke up and chased him out of the house. This woman had lived in this home for the past 40 years and had never had anything like this happen in the neighborhood.

So many more examples and experiences I would like to share, but my point is that having any type of security system is better than nothing. No matter what size family or home you have, having a security system monitoring your home is essential.

With the opioid epidemic and the state of the economy, burglars are becoming bolder, looking for money for their next fix. Break-ins occur every 20 seconds in the country, and usually happen during the day when the homeowner is at work or school. Burglars don't usually want any confrontation with homeowners, but that thinking is changing.

I've seen metal front doors kicked in so hard that there was a footprint indented in the bottom half of the door, and the interior doorjamb ripped off so hard that it landed at the other end of the hall entrance. Windows broken and ripped out, basement bulkhead doors broken into, and even large holes drilled into garage doors to get access to the home.

Again, you don't have to have an extremely expensive alarm system. Just have some type of service that watches over your family and your home when you're not home or sleeping.

Alarm systems come in various types, sizes, and levels of complexity. The type of system you choose will determine the cost of the installation and monthly monitoring fees. If you're just starting out with your first home and have a small budget for security, you have a few options. You can either contact a security company who can design and set up a system for you, or you can design your own system. Usually, wireless systems are the best way to go in existing homes due to the ease of installation and programming.

If the home you purchased has an existing alarm system, you may want to ask how old it is and who monitors it. Some systems can be adaptable to the existing system and save you a substantial amount of money. Also, most insurance companies give you a small discount off your homeowners insurance.

If the home has a hardwired security system, the windows have the sensors inside the lower windowsill. If a burglar knows that the home has a security system (usually houses that have security systems display signs and stickers), and if they can't see a wireless sensor between the upper and lower sash, they know not to open the lower sash and concentrate on lowering the upper sash to avoid activating the alarm. In cases like this we would always suggest upgrading the system to adapt it to wireless sensors between the two sashes to cover both the lower and upper sash of the window.

If the home does not have a security system, completely wireless is the way to go. If a security system representative comes to your house, make sure you do your homework and pick a system that can grow with your future needs to keep your family safe.

The following is a list of preferred entry points for burglars to enter your home or condo: front door, back door, sliders, basement, garage (both main and side doors), basement bulkhead doors, second-floor windows, attic vents (if reachable), and crawl spaces.

Let's use a ranch style home as our first example. Arming all the windows and doors on the first floor and basement is highly recommended. Also, a motion detector should be installed on both levels. These motion detectors can either be active or inactive depending on the arming of the system. Most systems have a "stay mode" which allows you to arm all the windows and doors while you are home. It allows you to walk around your home without setting off the alarm system and still protects you from intruders.

You also have an available "away mode" which arms all the windows, doors, and motion detectors. If you have any pets, most motion detectors are pet friendly and would allow your pet to move freely around the home without setting them off. Check with your installer or the company you purchase the system from as to the limit of the weight and size of the pet.

If the house has a large picture window, then a glass break sensor should be added to your system. This detector is designed to work with both modes mentioned and is vital if you have a set of sliding or French doors in your home. The detector will go off if anyone attempts to break in, even if they don't enter the home and don't set off the motion detector (such as a rock thrown through a window).

These examples from a ranch style house can easily be expanded to a larger home. I would just suggest arming the second floor, especially in the back and side windows of the home.

I've had a few homeowners resist in arming the home's second floor due to the additional cost. I took them outside and showed them how easy it was for a burglar to climb up to the second floor, especially when the homeowners leave an extension ladder lying down at the side of the house. Trash cans, air conditioning condensers, and trees are also easy ways to get to that second floor.

Every monitored alarm system I have seen has an emergency system built into the control panel (again, confirm this with your security company). When these buttons are pushed (either for fire or police), the monitoring center receives the message and contacts the local authorities first because time is of the essence. The monitoring center will then contact you for more information regarding your emergency.

When you stop and realize how important this monitored system is, it's much easier to justify the monthly monitoring charge. If you have a family with small children, teenagers, or even elders, the cost to protect them daily may be less than a dollar!

Smoke detectors and carbon monoxide detectors would be the next recommended level of protection for you and your family. Depending on your local fire prevention laws, both smoke and carbon monoxide protection must be installed and inspected prior to you owning and moving into your home. The only problem with this is that, if there is a fire in your home and you're not home, only your neighbors or passersby will notice the smoke billowing out of the home after it's fully engulfed in flames. By that time, the home will be a total loss, all your worldly possessions will be gone, and any pets inside the home will have perished.

Monitored smoke and carbon monoxide detectors are designed to protect your home whether you're in or out of your home. Over 500,000 pets die every year due to carbon monoxide and house fires. That alone should be a motivator to get a monitored system.

It doesn't matter if you're located in a "safe" neighborhood or a high crime area; video cameras strategically placed in and around your home are the next level of security. Video surveillance will give you great peace of mind and the ability to see anyone who may be a threat to your family and home. Depending on the type of system you decide to install, a notification could be sent to your home when one of your cameras is activated.

One of my clients had a raised ranch, also referred to as a split level depending on where you're from. His master bedroom was in the opposite end of the home from where the garage was located. His concern was knowing when his children returned home late at night after working late or being out on the town with their friends. His peace of mind was getting that notification from his phone that his children had arrived home safely. Also, he traveled a lot and still received that same notification on his phone when his children and wife arrived home safe and sound.

Remote activation on your smartphone allows you to turn your system on or off, lock or unlock doors, check on cameras with live feeds, and even know if someone is in your home and opens or closes a window or door.

3. *Additional Safety Tips*

- Having proper flashlights around your home, especially near the entrances and garages, will help keep you and your family safe. The basic inexpensive flashlights are usually around 100 lumens. 100 lumens can partially blind a person in darkness, but it takes a flashlight that produces at least 300 lumens to partially blind a person in the daylight. I highly recommend getting flashlights that produce at least 300 lumens and make sure the batteries are charged or replaced at least once a year.

- If you ever hear a baby crying outside your home, do not open your door. You may be being lured out of your home by either a burglar or attacker. Always call 911 and report the situation and wait for the police to arrive.

- If you hear a baby crying near you in a parking lot, you are probably being lured into being attacked and/or abducted. If no one else is around, go back into the store to get security involved and call 911 to handle this situation.

- Always keep your vehicle's windows closed and doors locked wherever you are. Your registration and insurance information are usually kept in the glove compartment and include your address and personal information.

- I also recommend that even if you park your car in the garage (attached or detached), keep the windows up and doors locked. Many garages are broken into, and your personal information is now at risk.

- While most thieves and burglars do their work during the day, they also work under the cover of darkness during the night. They very rarely burglarize a home that is well lit. Investing in motion detection exterior lighting is always a great idea.

4. Safe Landscaping

The two pictures above show some beautiful landscaping work. Both look great but the differences regarding you and your family's safety are very different.

The picture on the right allows burglars and attackers a place to hide and take cover. Having high shrubbery away from the house is dangerous but having these high shrubs against the house is even more dangerous.

Now I'm sure you're going to say, "When I get home, I stay in my car, drive into the garage and close the door." Burglars and other criminals who may have been watching your home know this and make plans to hide behind those shrubs close to the garage door. As soon as your car gets into the garage, they run in and hide in the garage as the door is closing. If they're smart enough, they'll step over the garage sensor that automatically reverses the garage door.

Other things that burglars look for are unkept lawns, overgrown shrubs, and accumulation of newspapers and mail. You should also have a clean line of sight to all sides of your property from all your windows and doors. Doing this makes your yard much safer against both two-legged and four-legged intruders.

If you're concerned about Peeping Toms, putting crushed rock in your gardens is recommended because it always makes noise when walked on. We have a pool in our backyard surrounded by a gravel walkway. This way we can always hear if someone comes around the corner.

I was driving down a busy street and saw this at the end of a driveway. I was so intrigued that I had to stop, turn around, and take a picture of it. Hundreds of cars go past this site until the trash is picked up. What concerns me is that hundreds of drivers now know that this family has a brand new 42-inch Samsung television. If any of these people were looking for a new television, they now know where to get one.

I highly recommend that people cut up these boxes and put them in the recycle or trash bins. Don't advertise what you purchase!

5. *Fire Prevention & Fire Escape Plans*

So many books and articles have been written for fire prevention, but not too many focus on fire escape plans. Having designed smoke and carbon monoxide systems for many homes, I can share with you the importance of having fire escape plans and the importance of practicing them with your family.

While working alongside the local fire department for over 38 years, many bad experiences were shared with us. From motor vehicle accidents to house fires, so many lives were lost due to mistakes made by people young and old.

One such experience was a family that decided to remove hot ashes from a woodstove, place them inside a plastic container, and leave it in the garage while they went out to dinner. They arrived home to a house fully engulfed in flames and a total loss. You would think that the average person would put such embers in a noncombustible metal container, but people just get complacent and think "this won't happen to us."

When I was around 10 years old, our neighbor wasn't watching her set of four-year-old twins as she should have been. They were outside playing and locked themselves inside the family car. They then decided to play with the cigarette lighter and started to burn the upholstery. Within minutes the car was in flames and both children perished in the fire.

In 2008, a family went out to dinner and returned home to find the house had smoke coming from the basement. Luckily a neighbor noticed the smoke and called the fire department, who was on-site in minutes. The fire took the life of a few family pets, but a cat and a dog were rescued. The fire was determined to be caused by a blocked clothes dryer. Not taking care of cleaning out your lint traps and dryer hoses can cause a fire to start very quickly due to the high heat of the dryer. Also, you should never run a dryer when you are not home. Approximately 2,900 dryer fires are reported every year in the US, resulting in approximately five deaths, 100 injuries, and over $35 million in property damage.

Research shows that, 30 years ago, the average time to escape a burning home was 17 minutes. As of now, that time has been reduced to three to four minutes. You would think that the time to escape a burning home would have increased due to stricter building codes and fire blocking, but the synthetic furniture and materials used in home construction actually burn hotter and faster than natural materials.

When you purchase new furniture and rugs, they have that "new car smell" so you can always tell that they were recently installed. This smell is called an "off gas" that slowly dissipates into the walls, ceilings, and flooring. When a fire gets started in the home, the off gases come back out and cause the fire to get hotter and burn faster. This is why an escape plan is very important for everyone in the home. The escape plan depends on what style house you own. Knowing what exits to use for each member of the family is important. Also, every pet should have a designated person to make sure they get out of the house safely. Finally, the escape plan should also include a meeting area far enough away from the home to escape the heat of the flames. Usually, a mailbox or utility pole is used for a safe meeting spot for the family.

Again, I hate to repeat myself, but practicing your fire escape plan creates "muscle memory." When stressful situations happen such as a home invasion or house fire, this muscle memory is very important to have. Practice...Practice...Practice!!

If you have an elderly person living with you, your situation will change constantly as time goes on in the care of these elders. Being in the situation that the child now takes care of the parents, you have concerns that your elders will be safe when you're not at home. You're considering getting them fall pendants in case they lose their balance. What happens when the fire department shows up to rescue your elders and they have no access to the home? Since they have no access to the home, they will use axes and other tools to break through the front door. You also must be concerned that, if your elders are taken to the hospital, your home is now open and accessible to anyone that walks by or follows the firetruck or EMS to your home.

One way to avoid this situation is to have remote door locks installed that you can access through your smartphone. These can be found at your local big box stores and are also available through most security alarm companies. They are a good way to allow house-keepers, dog walkers, or family members into your home; you can lock the doors after they enter or exit the home. But as always, they have certain limitations and chances of failure during an emergency.

On most multi-unit residential buildings and commercial buildings is an exterior lockbox (usually referred to by the name brand "KnoxBox," but others are available throughout the US). In case of an emergency when the building is locked down, this box allows the local fire department access to the building without damaging the doors or glass to gain entrance. Just for the fun of it, next time you go to any store or restaurant look for the KnoxBox.

The way it works on all multi-unit residential and commercial buildings is that whenever you want to change a lock in the building, the fire department is called to exchange a key in the KnoxBox. The fire department will use the key issued by the lockbox company, which is only usable in their city or town. No other community can use this key. The system is designed and located on the fire truck or ambulance and an access code needs to be entered before the lockbox key is accessible. This way the keys can be monitored by the user's code and can be traced if necessary.

The same company, the Knox Company, now offers what they call a "HomeBox." This box is much smaller and attaches directly to your home in any location you desire. The HomeBox key works the same way as it does in the multi-unit residential and commercial buildings. This HomeBox can be ordered online for a one-time fee very reasonably for under $200.00. The lockbox is made of three-quarter-inch steel so an acetylene torch would have to be used to gain access to the key inside the box. If an acetylene torch was used, by the time a burglar cut through the metal, the key inside would have melted and become unusable.

Why would you want to use a HomeBox instead of a remote door access or hide-a-key? Remote door access locks can fail if the batteries are not kept charged or periodically changed. The cold weather can also reduce the power level of the batteries, making the remote access unusable.

The "hide-a-key" method has many flaws that people are not aware of. The first thing burglars look for is the key under the mat. The second is in the flowerpot or flowerbed by the front door. If you decide to use the hide-a-key method, at least work it out with your neighbor so that you can hide your house key somewhere in their yard or shed.

Either way, in case of an emergency, the hide-a-key system will not stop the fire department or any EMS from breaking down the front door to get to an emergency inside your home.

6. Fire Extinguishers

Having fire extinguishers in your home is extremely important and knowing how to use them is even more important.

I was on a road trip on a major highway with my son Ryan, and we needed to make a pit stop. When we pulled off the highway into a large rest stop, I noticed that smoke was coming up from a row of shrubs located right near the gas pumps. I knew that someone had decided to throw their lit cigarette into the shrubs which lit the mulch on fire. I walked into the gas station store and asked the clerk (a young lady) behind the counter if she knew the shrubs were on fire. Of course, her answer was no. I then asked if she had a fire extinguisher, and her response was, "What's that!"

I told her that a fire extinguisher is usually red in color with a black hose coming out of the top. She went out back and found one and just looked at me with a blank stare. I asked if she knew how to use one and her response was a quick no. I grabbed it, pulled the safety pin out, went out and put out the fire.

I went back in and told the clerk to let her manager know that this extinguisher was now used and needed to either be replaced or recharged. Also, I told her that the manager needed to show all the employees how to use it.

An engineering and machine shop I used to work for decided to review all the safety procedures with the employees at their monthly meeting. I shared this story with the owner, and they included how to use an extinguisher in the company training.

Fire extinguishers come in a wide variety of sizes and shapes. Most of them look like the one shown above. The fire extinguishers recommended for residential use are called A-B-C fire extinguishers.

- Class A is primarily for wood, paper, and fabric.
- Class B is primarily for flammable liquids such as gasoline and oil-based products.
- Class C is primarily for electrical fires.

Some manufacturers also now label the extinguishers with numbers in front of the class rating.

For example:

- 10-B:C extinguisher would be able to handle a 25-square-foot fire.
- 5-B:C extinguisher would be able to handle a 12.5-square-foot fire.

Most extinguisher manufacturers recommend that you have at least one fire extinguisher on each floor of the house. One in the kitchen, which should be placed away from the stove because the first thing you're going to do is back away from the stove fire so on an opposite wall works best; one in the laundry room (in case of a dryer vent fire); and one in the garage for obvious reasons.

I would highly recommend that when you decide to purchase fire extinguishers for your home, you purchase one extra. Take that extra extinguisher and take your family outside away from any structure or landscaping. Take a piece of wood and rocks and make a fake fire pit, stand upwind and have each member of your household practice using it.

If you decide not to get the extra extinguisher, at least have each family pick up an extinguisher and practice using it with the safety pin still in place. Also, each family member should look at online videos to reinforce what they've just learned.

On another note, fire extinguishers have been known to disable unwanted visitors (two-legged and four-legged).

7. Fire Blankets

Fire blankets are used to extinguish fires in the kitchen (cooking oils, fats, and waste bins), and clothing fires. Covering the fire with the fire blanket cuts off the oxygen supply needed to fuel the fire. Fire blankets can only be used on Class A, B, and C fires.

20

IN-HOME DANGERS

During my many years as a police officer, childcare provider, certified home inspector, landlord, builder, and general contractor, I'm sure you can imagine what scenarios and situations I've seen with what people and their families have gotten themselves into.

I've seen nine-volt batteries taken out of smoke detectors because they were needed for remote controls by children. Sometimes, the children don't even tell the parents until something happens, and the detectors are no longer working. Usually, firefighters are the ones that discover this after the fire is put out. Now they must recover bodies and have police officers notify next-of-kin.

I've seen a house burnt to the ground because the homeowners decided to place embers from their fireplace inside a plastic bucket and go out for dinner. When they arrived home, their house was fully engulfed in flames and the home was a total loss.

One of the children who attended the childcare center I owned and operated fell out of a second-story window because the parent wasn't paying attention. The child pushed out the window screen and fell into a pile of shrubs. The child was okay with minor bruises but was very shaken up.

Times have certainly changed regarding gun safety and storage. Back in the late 1980s me and my family flew to Tennessee for a funeral. We stayed at my aunt's home and my boys were three and six years old. When we walked through the front door, I noticed a picture of a cowboy hanging over the couch. What really caught my eye was the gun belt stuck out from the picture; it looked as if it was holding an actual gun. I asked my aunt if that gun was real, and she said it was a .38-caliber pistol which was loaded. I asked her why she had it there and she said that the local prison was just a few miles away. She wanted to be ready if they escaped and decided to break into her home. I very calmly asked her if she could find another place to put that while we were visiting so that the children would not get their hands on it.

So many choices are out there for gun safes to keep them out of the hands of children. I'm not going into this matter now but approximately 1,400 children still die by accidental shootings.

Even with so much information out there on the internet regarding how to childproof your home, over 800,000 are rushed to the emergency room every year due to some type of poisoning. Poisoning can be caused by carbon monoxide, pesticides, cleaning products, pharmaceuticals, illegal drugs, personal care products, and even batteries. Poisons can be ingested by swallowing, inhaling, and chemicals passing through the skin.

Even if you don't have any children, your family and friends may have their own children. Being the homeowner, you are now responsible for anyone who visits or does any work in your home. If something happens to anyone inside the home, you are now opening yourself up for a situation that could have been avoided. Taking the proper steps when you move into your new home and continuing this routine of protecting anyone from encountering these products while in your home is a great habit to get into.

1. Carbon Monoxide

Carbon monoxide is the number one cause of poisoning in the US.

Carbon monoxide gas, also known as the "silent killer," is a gas you can't taste, smell, or see. Approximately 500 people die every year due to over exposure. Twenty thousand people are hospitalized every year due to exposure of carbon monoxide.

Symptoms of exposure include flu-like symptoms, headache, nausea, and dizziness. Symptoms of overexposure include unclear thinking, weakening legs, loss of consciousness, then finally death. If you or your family experiences these symptoms, get out of the house immediately and call 911. As I stated earlier, you should have your meeting place already established and hopefully you and your family have practiced this during your family fire drills.

When the seasons are changing, weather can get colder. We're closing our windows, tightening up our homes, adding insulation, turning up our heating systems, and spending more time indoors. What we're also doing is containing the carbon monoxide gas possibly being generated in the home. So again, make sure those devices are in working order and that the batteries are changed when recommended.

A client of mine had me look at some construction proposals for their home. I went into the basement and immediately started to smell exhaust fumes. I asked if this smell was always noticeable in the basement and the owners said yes. I went into the room where the heating system was located, and the smell was much stronger. When I looked at the vent pipe, I noticed it had a dime-sized hole that had rotted through the aluminum pipe and was allowing the exhaust fumes to enter the room. The hole was not very noticeable to the homeowners because it was in the back of the piping.

I know that carbon monoxide is an odorless poisonous gas, but after talking with a chimney expert, he explained to me that the odorless gas is only produced by the burning of natural gas. That would explain why we can smell car exhaust and burning oil from vent pipes; both are considered carbon monoxide.

2. Humidity Levels

A client made an appointment to have their windows replaced because mold was constantly growing around the window glass and framing. I walked into the home and noticed that it was very humid. His family was very fond of fish and had about eight 20- to 40-gallon fish tanks throughout the home.

The normal humidity level in a home is between 30 and 50 percent. The humidity level in this home was around 80 to 90 percent, which was causing mold to grow around the windows and walls. After explaining this situation, I advised the client that, in order to have so many tanks creating this amount of humidity, they needed to install a dehumidifier to balance out the relative humidity.

Some newer heating systems have a built-in humidifier for the home which makes the home more comfortable in the wintertime. In some existing HVAC units, you can have your HVAC technician install a system to increase the home's humidity.

Air conditioning units are designed to remove the humidity from air in the home, which allows the air to cool to comfortable temperatures during the summer.

3. *Storage of Dangerous Chemicals*

GASOLINE

As with any other problem, the solution usually is addressed after an accident or death. In this case, we're talking about the storage of one of the leading causes of explosions in garages and sheds: gasoline.

Growing up in the 1960s and 1970s, all my neighbors and friends' parents had gas-powered lawnmowers. Those mowers were stored in either the garage or outdoor shed. There was no one out there to teach people that if you wanted to refill the gas tank on the mower, that you should not do it on a tarred driveway. Eventually everyone caught on that, when the gasoline tank overflowed, the spilled gasoline eventually would make a hole in the tar and continue to eat away at it, making big holes in the driveway. The next solution was to either refill the tank over the grass, and they eventually learned that the spilled gas would kill the grass.

Now in their infinite wisdom, everyone decided to fill the mower's gas tank inside their garages because the spilled gasoline did not bother the cement floor. They would just wipe up the spilled gasoline and put the gas soiled rag in the corner of the garage, setting themselves up for another fire hazard.

After the gas tank was filled and the excess wiped up off the mower and the floor, homeowners would start up their mowers and begin mowing the lawn around the home. Because the gas tanks really didn't hold much gas, the tanks had to be refilled a few times during this process. Then why do you need to put the cover on the gas can and keep it out of direct sunlight?

A gallon of gas weighs approximately 6.3 pounds, and as a liquid is nonflammable. The vapors from that gallon of gasoline are what can ignite if allowed to collect inside a small area such as a garage or outdoor shed. When a gallon of gas is fully vaporized inside an enclosed area, the explosive power is equal to 83 sticks of dynamite.

A friend of the family decided to refill his mower's gas tank inside the outdoor shed while the mower was red hot. The shed was full of gas fumes; the mower exploded and caused severe burns on most of his body.

Again, nothing is ever resolved until someone gets hurt or dies! Well, portable gas tanks have come a long way:

All these metal gas cans once performed a great service for both residential and commercial uses back in their days. Everything was going well, until someone realized that when you keep these gas cans open and the vapors escape, if anything struck the metal can, a small spark could cause the vapors surrounding the can to ignite. Outside of the fatalities and personal injuries, many garages, sheds, houses, barns, and businesses have suffered severe damage or total losses due to gasoline explosions. So how do we remedy this?

After many generations of different types of plastic containers, they now offer a spill-proof plastic gas container. This container

only works when the container is turned upside down, and the nozzle is placed inside the fuel tank. Pressure must then be applied to the nozzle for the gasoline to be dispersed. This new way to dispense the gasoline is much safer because it reduces the chance of spilling gas, and it stays closed when the nozzle is not dispensing fuel.

Always make sure that you store your gasoline cans in an outdoor shed away from the home. If this is not possible and if you must leave it in the garage (again, I suggest you don't), make sure that the container is completely sealed, and no vapors are escaping. Also, never leave the gasoline can out in direct sunlight because the gasoline vapors will expand inside the tank. If the vapors expand enough within the container, it may cause the container to rupture and allow vapors to escape and create a major hazard.

I've owned many lawnmowers, tractors, trimmers, and even chainsaws. It's nice to have all these tools when you're living in your own home, but with these tools comes more routine maintenance. Having a job, family responsibilities, and time constraints make it difficult to keep up with routine maintenance. I've lost count as to how many engines have died or I couldn't get started. I always end up replacing them because it is cheaper than getting them repaired.

It took a few years and many thousands of dollars before I realized that electric or battery-operated tools last much longer than tools with gasoline-powered engines (depending on how well you take the time to maintain them). Also, I don't have to deal with storing and dispensing gasoline. These tools were not as available as they are now and are at a much lower price. You can't always go completely electric, but you may want to consider this before you go on that buying spree at your local hardware or big box store.

Just a funny story to share: I grew up in a rural community of about 12,000 people. While clearing land and needing my chainsaws resharpened, I met a guy who lived close to the center of town and visited him often to resharpen my chainsaws. While waiting for my haircut from the barber located in the town center, I looked out the window and noticed this same guy driving his lawn tractor through the center of town. Many other guys in the barber shop joined me in laughing at this event, but he was eventually stopped by the local police. The police officer, who also knew him very well, started laughing and nicely asked him to ride the tractor back home and please don't do that again.

PROPANE TANKS

Why do you need a propane tank? Almost every household has an outdoor grill that usually works with propane gas. The one (or two) tanks are approximately 20 pounds and fit under or inside the grill. These tanks can be purchased and filled at many propane filling stations. The downside of owning your own propane tanks is that they are only good up to 10 years. After the 10 years are over, the propane filling stations will no longer fill them due to liability reasons. Also, when you own your own propane tank, they can get very gross and dirty depending on where and when they're used. There are also services available that allow you to purchase the first tank that comes prefilled, and when it's empty you can switch out the tank for a new one. The best part of this is that you'll always have a pre-tested, clean, and fresh tank to put back in your grill.

Propane tanks come in a wide variety of sizes and weights depending on the homeowner's requirements. Depending on your neighborhood, natural gas lines may have been installed, and your home's heating system, hot water tanks, stoves, and fireplaces are run off natural gas. In some areas, natural gas lines may not have been installed in the streets due to too much ledge to dig and blast through. The alternative to having your home heated with oil is to have a larger propane gas tank located on the property.

Some homes use various different types of fuel. Homes that use oil for heating may want to use gas for cooking. It all comes down to personal preference and there's absolutely nothing wrong with using different types of fuel in the home. One of the last houses I built, natural gas was not available on the street. I wanted to have gas fireplaces in my house, so I just added the smaller tanks to the back of the house—usually 100- to 200-pound tanks. These tanks expire after 12 years and can either be replaced or re-inspected every five years.

Homeowners who want to stay with propane for use in all their appliances and heating systems must use a much larger tank that holds anywhere from 500 to 1,000 pounds of propane. These tanks take up a lot of space and are sometimes located further away from the house and surrounded by some type of shrubbery or fencing to help hide them. The piping is run underground and into the home. Depending on where your home is located, there may be no place to put this tank where it won't stick out like a sore thumb. These tanks can also be placed underground so that they can be totally hidden from view. The only downside of burying these tanks is that you'll never know what condition the tank is in, and their life expectancy is between 20 to 30 years. I'm sure the cost to have it removed and another put in its place would be very expensive.

Just FYI, a path must always be cleared to all these home propane tanks so that the delivery service can refill them. If the paths are not clear, especially from snow, the delivery service will not deliver the propane and you may just run out. Not a good thing to happen, especially in the winter!

OIL TANKS

Using oil for home heating is another alternative and newer burners utilize this fuel much more efficiently. Oil tanks come in a variety of sizes depending on the size of the home and the current needs of the homeowner. At the top of the tank, you'll see a fill pipe (lower) and the vent pipe (upper), and you'll usually find the oil level gauge located on the vent stack. Oil tanks are usually located in the basement of the home, but for slab houses the tanks are either located in the garage or outside of the home.

With natural gas and electrical heating systems, both come into the home, via piping or through the electrical panel. With oil tanks, a path must always be cleared during all seasons so that the oil delivery service can locate and fill your tank. If the tank is blocked, especially with snow, the delivery service may not deliver the oil and you may run out. Just another thing to add to your "to do" list, especially if you are on a routine delivery schedule.

Care must always be taken when working around these fuel tanks. The copper tubing is not always heavy-duty piping and may be easily damaged if something heavy is dropped on it. Where the fuel flows out of the tank is a filter to remove any sediment that may have come from the tank. It's a good habit to have this oil filter changed annually, usually at the time you have your oil heating system cleaned. There is a shutoff valve before the filter and sometimes it leaks. You may see some kitty litter or other type of absorbent material there to capture drips from changing the filter.

Things to watch out for include any rust on the tank, and it usually will start around the bottom. Some tanks have an oil pan underneath to capture any leaking oil and a monitor can be purchased to let you know your tank may be leaking. Once again, your home inspector will inspect the tank, but it's still good for you to have this knowledge.

When I owned my school, we had to move our oil tank to another location inside the basement due to needed renovations. My friend, who owned an oil and burner service company, highly recommended that we remove the old filling and venting pipes or at least fill them with cement.

Another colleague of his said that one of his employees went to a client's house and the homeowners did not inform the oil service company that they relocated the tank and put in new fill and vent pipes on the other side of the house.

The employee went to the old location of the fill pipe, hooked up the oil hose, and began pumping oil into the open basement.

The employee finally realized that the tank should have been filled, but he still had not heard the whistle which the vent pipe makes to let the employee know that the tank was full. Long story short, over 300 gallons of oil was pumped into the basement.

The cost to remove those 300 gallons, clean up the area, jack-hammer the cement, excavate the contaminated oil, put back clean fill, and re-cement the basement floor was in excess of $30,000. The homeowner's oil service company and the homeowner's insurance company now had to fight on whose liability this was and who was going to pay for it.

All of this could have been avoided if the homeowner had just contacted the oil delivery service and told them where the new piping was located. Also, it would be a good idea to remove or fill the piping with cement just in case the delivery person didn't get the message. Just a good story to share in case you're thinking of doing any renovations and need to relocate your oil tank!

POOL CHEMICALS

If your new home has either an in-ground or aboveground pool, chemicals need to be used to keep the water sparkling clean and safe. There are a few different ways to keep your pool water clean and safe for your family. Chlorine is the most commonly used and it comes in tablets, powder, or liquid form. Other chemicals include bromine and Baquacil. There are also saltwater purifiers and reverse ionization systems.

If the former owner used chlorine, storing this chemical properly is of vital importance. The CDC reports:

*During 2015—2017, **pool chemical injuries** led to an estimated 13,508 U.S. emergency department visits, approximately one third of which occurred in persons aged <18 years. Most **injuries** occurred at a residence, and two thirds occurred* *during the summer swimming season (Memorial Day weekend through Labor Day).*

Most harmful chlorine exposures are the result of inhalation. Health effects typically begin within seconds to minutes. Following chlorine exposure, the most common symptoms are airway irritation, wheezing, difficulty breathing, sore throat, cough, chest tightness, eye irritation, and skin irritation.

If chlorine is not covered and stored properly, chlorine gas can form in enclosed areas. Chlorine gas is heavier than air and stays close to the ground, causing other hazards like fire and possible explosions.

21

SICK HOUSE SYNDROME

A few required courses I took to become a certified home inspector were on mold, water intrusion, and relative humidity levels. Your home inspector is only limited to what they can see, and not what is behind the home's walls.

One of my clients had just purchased a home in Boston and wanted to have an alarm system installed. He was undergoing renovations at the time, and we had to locate the existing system in the basement to see just what had to be done to replace the system. I noticed a very heavy mold smell in the basement and after about five minutes my eyes began watering. I started coughing and having a hard time breathing. We immediately left the basement and went out into open air. After having a drink of water and getting some fresh air, it took about 15 minutes before the symptoms subsided. He informed me that they were in the process of removing the old carpeting in the basement, which might have caused all that mold to become airborne.

As I've stated earlier, your home is a living breathing organism that needs proper ventilation. Your home is exposed to the weather 24/7/365 and must adjust to all the temperature and humidity levels outside *and* inside. Just remember that when hot meets cold, moisture is made. That moisture needs a place to go and that includes through the walls to the outside air. Most paints and stains allow this transfer of moisture but sealing up your home with any new type of siding like vinyl may stop that transfer of moisture. If you look closely at vinyl siding, it has small weep holes to allow the moisture to escape.

Having an environmentally safe home for you and your family is extremely important. Depending on the age of a home, proper building codes during the time of construction may not have been in place to reduce "Sick House Syndrome."

If you look at a loaf of bread that has been around for a few weeks, it will start to develop mold and needs to be thrown out. So, if the mold can grow inside a closed bag, what do you think it can do inside your home's walls, ceilings, basements, and even the ductwork?

Possible symptoms of Sick House Syndrome include throat irritation; breathing difficulties; tightness in the chest; runny nose; allergy-like symptoms such as sneezing; burning sensations in the nose; dry, itchy skin rashes; headaches; dizziness; difficulty concentrating; forgetfulness; fatigue; irritability; nausea; body aches; fever; and chills. Some of these symptoms may be the result of other allergies, or in my case the irritability is just my own personality (as my wife would say).

22

SEVERE WEATHER

When I worked for a construction company, one of my client's homes was struck by lightning. I have never experienced such damage to a home.

There was a wire dog run that ran from the side entrance of the home to a very old and healthy oak tree. The tree was struck by lightning and the electrical current passed down to the dog run, jumped from the dog run to the home, jumped to the home's electrical service, and followed that wire into the attic where it ended at a light fixture. The current was still so strong it blew a two-foot hole through the roof and daylight now lit up the attic. The oak tree had a scar on the bark that resembled the exact size and shape of the wire. It heated the wire up so much that it scarred the bark when it snapped back from the house. Seeing this—I know it's rare—I always recommend that people don't connect any metal dog runs to the home as you're now making a conductor for a lightning strike.

A security client had his backup generator struck by lightning. The generator was about 50 feet away from the house along the tree line. The lightning hit a tree and followed it to the wiring in the ground, and over to the home's electrical service. The current was so strong that it destroyed the electrical service panel, along with many appliances and household fixtures.

Another security client had a tree in his backyard struck by lightning. It broke the tree in half, and the current flowed underground and into the home through the water line. It jumped to the electrical service panel and destroyed the panel, and again, many appliances and household fixtures.

The stories shared above were rare lightning strikes, but they still could happen to your home. There is not much you can do to prevent lightning strikes from following electrical lines or piping into the home, but you can better your odds by not installing things like dog runs and other metal attachments that act as conductors.

I'm always watching the weather, especially when storms are approaching or developing, and I also recommend everyone else do the same.

When I purchased my boat back in the early 1990s, I decided to take the navigation and boating safety courses offered by the U.S. Coast Guard Auxiliary. During these courses, it was ingrained in us to purchase marine weather radios and to listen to the weather prior to going out on the water, and to continue listening the entire time you're out. If you're out in open water and a storm develops, you have nowhere to go. You have to hope and pray that you can get back to your marina or boat ramp before you're in danger. I have seen skies and seas turn ugly very fast, so planning your trip around the weather will help you avoid these dangerous situations.

Having learned this information about severe weather, it really came in handy when I had my school. I was working outside on the grounds of the school and the children were playing in the playgrounds. While out there, the sky went from blue to black very quickly. I looked up and saw what looked like an anvil in the sky, and instantly knew that this was two weather fronts colliding. I immediately told all the teachers to get the children back in the school. Within minutes thunder, lightning, and torrential rains were right over us and all the children and staff were safely inside the building.

Having a home on land does offer the protection you need to stay safe, but knowing when storms are approaching, and their severity, is still very important. Outdoor furniture, tents, canopies and even grills may need to be secured to prevent any damage to the objects or the home.

There is so much information on the web to show you how to keep you and your family safe during severe weather, so I won't go into any further details at this time.

23

FLOODS AND NATURAL DISASTERS

In April of 2015, the northeast section of the United States was hit with the 100-year flood. In my 63 years of life, this was the worst flood I have seen firsthand in my life. I'm very aware of other parts of the country having severe flooding, hurricanes, tornadoes, thunder, and lightning strikes, but I've never seen them firsthand.

My wife and I have been together for over 14 years, and we both agree that we have never seen such escalation of the number of storms and their increasing intensity throughout our entire lifetimes. Over the past few years, we've had some severe storms pass over our home that actually shook the windows, along with flooding rains.

We have the ability to watch and monitor the weather patterns with applications right on our phones because of all the new and improved satellites, which makes it easier to prepare and protect our homes and family. It just seems like we're experiencing more hurricanes, tornadoes, and earthquakes.

In closing, just be aware of the weather and keep you and your family safe!

24

SUMMARY

When the decision is made to start looking for a home, find a reputable and experienced real estate agent.

When I teach safety seminars for real estate agents, I highly recommend that the agent has their future client meet them at their office where they are safe and protected. Fully vet the new client and get all the relevant names and information. I highly recommend that you (the future potential client) do the same with the real estate agent.

Explain what type of home you're looking for and what city or town you're looking to move too.

When you find the home you're looking for, make sure you do your homework and due diligence. When you walk around the home's interior and exterior, take the information you just learned and don't be afraid to ask as many questions as you need to make you comfortable.

After the offer is made and accepted, hire an experienced *certified and licensed home inspector*. Make sure you talk to the inspector and verify that both you and your real estate agent are allowed to follow them through the entire inspection. Again, don't be afraid to ask as many questions as you need to make you comfortable. Take that information regarding deficiencies in the home you received from the home inspector; it now becomes a negotiation tool for your real estate agent. Negotiations should be made on whether the homeowner will fix the deficiencies or take the price of getting the deficiencies repaired off the price of the home. Ask your agent how they wish to proceed with this situation.

If the home has a boiler, burner, or even an HVAC system, I always suggest that you have a specialist come in and analyze the system. Home inspectors have a lot of knowledge in these systems, but it is not their specialty. We were strongly advised not to run air conditioning systems in the winter or any type of heating system in the summer because of possible damages to the systems.

If the home has an older brick chimney, I highly recommend that you again hire a specialist to make sure the chimney is intact, and no cracks are in the interior flue chamber. Home inspectors are taught to view certain areas of fireplaces and burner flues, but again I still highly recommend spending the money in advance to hire a professional chimney sweep and get a separate inspection.

If the home has a water well, I'm sure your real estate agent will instruct you to get a well inspection since home inspectors don't usually do this.

If the home has a leaching system, again I'm sure your real estate agent will instruct you to get the system checked and pumped. Usually, the seller pays for this inspection.

Your real estate agent will also suggest that you get a radon test. Get this done early so you'll get the results back within your 7-to-10-day due diligence time.

Make sure you visit your future neighborhood during different times of the day. Also, see what commercial industries, highways, and railways are near your new neighborhood. I would even recommend you do this prior to putting in an offer to purchase the home.

Closing on the home (paperwork, money, and property exchange) is usually a very happy event. Sometimes certain paperwork may be missing and cause a delay in the closing. Be patient and it will happen. Stay in contact with your agent to see when it will be rescheduled. At the closing you will receive keys to your new home (again, I highly recommend you change the locks on all entry doors when you move in).

Moving in is very tedious backbreaking work, but also a very enjoyable and exciting day. Make sure you hire a credible moving company and that they put the properly marked boxes inside the room where they will be unpacked.

If you're moving yourself, organization of the move will make it much smoother and less stressful.

After you get everything into your new home, set up the beds and other furnishings, take a break and celebrate your new home!

Now is the time you and your family will start to understand how your home runs and what noises come from appliances, heating/cooling systems, and outdoors (if any).

Focusing on your family's security should be your next concern. Do your homework and get just a basic system that you can expand on as your family progresses.

We covered meeting neighbors and exchanging contact information earlier.

CLOSING

I wrote this book to help educate people on what to watch for when they start looking for their first or next home or condo. I also wrote this book to teach people how to be safe in their new home.

I hope this book has helped you, and I wish you well on your search for a SAFE & HEALTHY HOME.

In my next book *Dangerous Life—Dangerous Living*, I will teach you and your family additional home safety strategies as well as how to be safe while at home, commuting, working, shopping, and on vacations.

I have seen many people put their lives in danger, most of which could have been avoided. Be prepared, stay safe, and enjoy the journey of owning your new home!

Made in the USA
Middletown, DE
04 March 2022

62052308R00086